Praise for *The Great Formula*

"With the right formula you can create dynamite and explode things. With this formula you can create sales and make more money than ever before. Which do you want?"
—Joe Vitale, Author of *The Attractor Factor*

"This book reminds me of Isaac Newton's discovery of gravity— **a stunningly simple idea that changed the course of history**. I've seen The Great Formula create millionaires with surprising speed. **It's an exact recipe to turn a marginal business into a successful one.** Even better, a successful business can ride this formula to stratospheric heights in short order."
—David Garfinkel, Author of
Customers on Demand

"Bringing the customer back for more is a key success principle. Mark Joyner shares not only his own immensely successful experience at this, but the wisdom of people who created worldwide brands out of nothing: from King Gillette, who created the entire disposable razor industry a century ago, to Amazon.com founder Jeff Bezos. Then he tops the package with 'how-I-did-it' articles from an amazing roster of today's hottest marketing superstars. If you can't learn something from this book, are you sure you're still breathing?"
—Shel Horowitz, Award-Winning Author of
Principled Profit: Marketing That Puts People First, www.frugalmarketing.com

"It never ceases to amaze me. Though it's been 10 years since Mark Joyner turned the marketing world on its ear with his incredibly inventive concepts and strategies, he continues to stay on the absolute cutting edge with *The Great Formula*. I consider Mr. Joyner a life-changing mentor and although I know I'm far from alone, our ranks will rise considerably once this book goes public."
—Mike Merz, JVNotifyPro.com

"An elegant, insightful, and amazing analysis of an elementary, yet critical tenet of marketing. By combining storytelling with case studies, and doing it in his typical captivating style, Mark Joyner has once again succeeded at coming up with an entertaining and educational marketing masterpiece. *The Great Formula* is what every aspiring entrepreneur must read and take to heart to succeed massively—with the least effort. Together with *The Irresistible Offer*, this book is all you need to start—and win—the selling game . . . whatever business you're in."
> —Dr. Mani Sivasubramanian, Infopreneur and
> Heart Surgeon, www.PositivePromise.com

"I find *The Great Formula* to be a work of magic. The reason I say that is because it is so simple when it is revealed to you, you almost want to scratch your head that you have been in business and not using the simple Great Formula. The reason I chose the word *magic* is because if you have ever seen a great magic trick, it blows your mind . . . until you are let in on the hidden secret to how it works. Then you say, 'Is that all there is to it? I can do that!' Such is true for The Great Formula, and if you do not know what it is, it could cost you dearly. The case studies in this book are mind-blowing to say the least and work in perfect harmony with *The Irresistible Offer*. I am excited to put it into action!"
> —Mike Filsaime, www.PayDotCom.com

"Mark Joyner's expectations to produce true masterpieces are hard for anyone to live up to, but he exceeds these expectations time and time again. **The Great Formula is the Holy Grail for every business's success.** If you want to break the barriers that have been holding you back from the success you know your business is capable of, get a copy for every employee you have and require them to master it. This is where you will find true success. Period."
> —Sam Heyer, CEO, Magga Marketing, Inc.,
> www.maggamarketing.com

"This book is a methodical dissection of what successful marketing is all about and abundantly makes *The Great Formula* accessible in this sure-footed guide to growing your business. It's insightful about human behavior, pragmatic, and powerful."

—Joe Soto, NLP Trainer,
www.PersuasionTraining.com

"Filled with simple truths, personal experiences, and the wisdom of some of the brilliant strategists in marketing, *The Great Formula* contains a wealth of commonsense solutions for almost every business challenge. Read it and you'll prosper."

—Joseph Sugarman, Chairman, BluBlocker
Corporation

"Mark Joyner is to The Great Formula as Albert Einstein is to E = MC². *The Great Formula* is a powerful, concise snapshot of the universal laws of marketing that reliably govern the velocity of revenue growth in your business. Using 30 case studies and articles, Mark convincingly teaches how the three core strategies and the dozen key tactics of *The Great Formula* can be applied in almost every conceivable business scenario to drive massive sales growth. Save yourself a couple of hundred thousand dollars on that degree. **Clear out your bookcase. The MBA curriculum for this generation is *The Irresistible Offer* and *The Great Formula*.**"

—Lou D'Alo, www.powerupcoaching.com

"These ideas have stood the test of time, but I've never seen them put so succinctly. Then, 21 case studies of exactly how Mark's formula has been applied successfully, ranging from start-ups to million-dollar enterprises. *The Great Formula* is street-smart: lean, scrappy, and powerful."

—Ben Mack, Author of *Poker Without Cards*;
Former Senior Vice President, BBDO; Brand
Strategy Director, Cingular

"*The Great Formula* is a masterpiece on wheels. Motivational . . . inspiring . . . scientifically proven."
—Jason and Skye Mangrum, Authors,
Consultants, e-Business Professionals,
www.JasonMangrum.com

"Mark Joyner is a master marketer in every sense, and with the wisdom and strategies of this book, he comes about as close as anyone will ever get to proactive marketing. Spend your last dime to get it if you have to, because *The Great Formula* is a must-have book."
—Randy "Dr. Proactive" Gilbert, Host of
The Inside Success Show

THE GREAT FORMULA

THE GREAT FORMULA

for Creating Maximum Profit with Minimal Effort

Mark Joyner

WILEY

John Wiley & Sons, Inc.

Published by John Wiley & Sons, Inc., Hoboken, New Jersey.
Published simultaneously in Canada.

For general information on our other products and services please contact our Customer Care Department within the U.S. at (800) 762-2974, outside the United States at (317) 572-3993 or fax (317) 572-4002.

Wiley also publishes its books in a variety of electronic formats. Some content that appears in print may not be available in electronic books. For more information about Wiley products, visit our web site at www.wiley.com.

Library of Congress Cataloging-in-Publication Data:

Joyner, Mark, 1968–
    The great formula : for creating maximum profit with minimal effort / Mark Joyner.
        p. cm.
    Includes index.
    ISBN-13: 978-0-471-77823-3 (cloth)
    ISBN-10: 0-471-77823-0 (cloth)
    1. Selling.   2. Success in business.   I. Title.
    HF5438.25.J696   2006
    658.85—dc22   2005034028

Printed in the United States of America.

10 9 8 7 6 5 4 3 2 1

CONTENTS

CONTENTS

Contents

xi

CONTENTS

CHAPTER 1

Introduction—
H × 2 + O

Two parts hydrogen plus one part oxygen.

That's the scientific formula for water.

What if there were such a formula for business success?

Would it not be easy to create a million-dollar empire?

Such a formula does exist, and it's called The Great Formula.

It's been around for years, and almost every great business success in history has used it.

Before I reveal this formula to you and how you can immediately apply it to your business for an instant increase in profitability, there is an important question we need to ask:

If this formula is so simple and so powerful, why doesn't every business use it?

Why are there so many business failures?

Read on. . . .

CHAPTER 2

"I Get 1,000 Channels of TV and Most of It's Crap"

The French physicist Emile Borel had an interesting theory.

He said: Take an infinite number of monkeys and put them all in front of typewriters. Eventually one will bang out the complete script for *Hamlet*.

It's popular among Web-heads to joke that "The advent of the blog has proven Borel wrong."

It is far easier now to produce information than ever before. Anyone with Internet access can publish information in blogs with the click of a mouse button.

Even print publishing is far easier now than it was even 10 years ago. The print-on-demand industry has allowed just about anyone with a computer to create and publish a printed work at very little cost.

One might be tempted to wax philosophical about how wonderful this is, but it presents a problem with which we're just barely coming to grips.

Just how quickly is the world body of information growing?

Very little definitive work has been done on the subject, but a commonly accepted estimate is that the world body of information *doubles* once every five years.

Is this true?

Well, no one seems to know for sure. I mean, how would you measure it?

The famous University of California at Berkeley School of Information Management and Systems (SIMS) tried to do just that. In 2003 SIMS produced a great piece of research called "How Much Information 2003."

In it, the researchers tried to determine just how much information there was in the world and estimate the rate at which it was growing.

They figured that in 1999 two to three exabytes of new information were created in all media (film, print, audio, you name it).

Wait a minute. . . .

What's an exabyte?

You've probably heard of megabytes and gigabytes, and if you're an übergeek you probably know what terabytes are, but *exa*btyes?

First, let's look at bytes.

Without getting too technical, a byte is roughly equivalent to a single alphanumeric character.

"Alphanumeric" simply means letters and numbers.

1

See that? That was about one byte.

Gorgonzola!

There go about 11 bytes.

A kilobyte is 1,000 bytes, just like a kilometer is 1,000 meters.

An *exa*byte is 10^{18} bytes.

That's 1,000,000,000,000,000,000 (one quintillion) bytes of information.

In 1999 the world cranked out somewhere between two and three of those bad boys, according to the folks at SIMS.

In 2002, they say, the world produced five exabytes of *new* information.

Every year, we're producing 35 percent more information than the year before.

Let's put this into perspective.

Kilobyte   1,000 bytes
1 kilobyte = one printed page

Megabyte   1,000,000 bytes
1 megabyte = one book

Gigabyte   1,000,000,000 bytes
1 gigabyte = a truckload of books

Terabyte   1,000,000,000,000 bytes
10 terabytes = the printed material in the Library of Congress

Petrabyte   1,000,000,000,000,000 bytes
200 petrabytes = all of the printed material in the world

Exabyte   1,000,000,000,000,000,000 bytes
5 exabytes = every word spoken by every person who ever lived

---

Is information doubling every five years? Is the rate at which it grows 30 percent faster each year?

I don't know about you, but this study lost me somewhere before terabytes.

Imagine . . .

If there were 1,000 books about business available 10 years ago, that would mean that there are 1,024,000 available today.

This is all rather exciting, but here's the rub. Although the quantity of new information is increasing rapidly, the overall quality may in fact be on the decline.

Ah, to heck with it. Let's just be blunt. The vast majority of new information available today is just plain rubbish.

And if it's not rubbish, it is probably so specialized that you'll never have any use for it.

So, how do business owners cope with this?

Every week they are faced with new books to read, new marketing theories, and new ideas.

A new way of handling information is needed. . . .

CHAPTER 3

Chunking

Have you ever wondered why phone numbers are seven digits long?

I mean, why not six? Or eight? Or 20?

Princeton University cognitive psychologist George Miller wrote a paper in 1956 titled "The Magical Number Seven, Plus or Minus Two: Some Limits on Our Capacity for Processing Information" (*Psychological Review* 63, 81–97).

In it, he observed that the human mind can hold only between five and nine units of information consciously at a time.

This seems to be a structural limitation for which we are hardwired.

This research subsequently influenced the current telephone numbering system. If phone numbers were longer than seven digits most people would have quite a hard time remembering them.

Someday we may hot-rod the mind and break past this limitation, but for now we must resort to dirty tricks.

The pseudoscientific field of mnemonics has created a number of useful tools we can use to trick our minds into storing more information than we should ordinarily be able to.

One of them, observed by Miller, is referred to as chunking.

It works like this. Trick the brain into thinking that a string of information is actually a single chunk and it will treat it as a single unit.

Let me give you an example.

Try to memorize the following string of digits.

Just read it once, close your eyes, and see if you can recall it in order.

1
1
4
1
1
9
4
8
9
1

2

9

4

1

Okay, great. How did you do?

Probably not so well. That's a string of 14 digits, and most people simply can't memorize such a string with a single glance.

The problem is, you're processing that string as 14 individual units and your brain is choking on the 7 +/– 2 barrier.

Let's trick your brain now and see what happens.

This time I want you to read the string **from bottom to top** and look at them in the groups I've created.

1

1

4

1

1

9

4

8

9

1

2

9

4

1

Now, pull out a piece of paper and see if you can write those 14 numbers in the exact order in which they appear on the page.

If you are European, you probably got at least eight of them (the bottom eight), and if you're American and fairly well read, you probably got the whole lot.

What was different this time?

This time you were able to chunk the numbers into individual groups. If you followed the instructions and read them from the bottom to the top, you probably would have recognized . . .

1
1
4 — 411—the number we call in the United States for information

1
1
9 — 911—the number we call in the United States in an emergency

4
8
9
1 — 1984—the title of a famous novel by George Orwell

2
9
4
1 — 1492—the year Christopher Columbus sailed the ocean blue

Try it again now. See if you can reproduce the entire string on a piece of paper.

This time, I don't think anyone reading will have failed to remember all 14 digits.

There. You just tricked your brain. Your brain remembered those 14 digits as a measly four chunks, so it was able to process them quite easily.

So, what place does this have in a book about business?

I'm assuming . . .

- You are human.
- You have a brain.
- You either run a business or have some pivotal role in running one.

If that's you, read on. . . .

CHAPTER 4

The Great Chunkula

We chunk data in other ways as well.

Hierarchical structures, rules, formulas . . . these are all ways to chunk information and make it more manageable.

Now, this chunking process doesn't affect just our rote memory—it also affects our behavior.

In a sense, a rule is a chunking method that allows you to prechunk situations and react to them accordingly.

Here's an odd example.

There is a burgeoning cottage industry in the art of the pick-up. Here, people like Neil Strauss, author of *The Game*, take dating-inept men and teach them how to be pick-up artists.

Most dismiss this as a sleazy practice of the lunatic fringe, but it's rapidly gaining in popularity. And, surprisingly, they actually teach some fairly useful rules as well.

One of the rules they teach their young would-be pick-up artists is the rule of the sh*t test.

When a man approaches a woman in whom he's interested, there are limitless ways she can respond.

Imagine you're a man trying to chat up a woman in a bar and she replies, "Did your mommy know you'd be out past your bedtime when she dressed you tonight?"

That's original. You've never heard that blowoff before.

Now, your average socially inept fellow might respond in one of several ways:

- Think seriously about what she said and try to answer. "Oh, well. Actually, my mom didn't dress me. I dressed myself. . . . What made you think my mom dressed me?"
- Realize that she's giving off negative signals and walk away.
- Get angry and defensive. "Oh yeah?! What do you know about it? You may be beautiful, but I bet you don't have a brain." (That'll teach her!)

A guy schooled in the way of "The Game" (the new industry's term for the art of the pick-up) would immediately identify her reply as a sh*t test and know how to reply.

These guys practice responding to sh*t tests and even swap response tactics. It's a science for them.

Interestingly, the pick-up artists think of these tests as positive things. If the woman was really not interested in you, she wouldn't be testing you. They theorize that these are tests of your social value, and how well you respond will determine your worthiness as a suitor.

Surprisingly sophisticated psychology!

The important thing to note here is that they have prechunked the data based on the rule they created and the effect is stunningly useful.

Rather than think on the spot about how to reply, you're 10 steps ahead of the game and immediately know what to do.

You do this exact same thing when you're at a four-way stop.

We have a rule that tells us, "Yield to the car that stops there first, and if you stop at the same time yield to the car on the right."

If we didn't have a set of prechunking rules we'd have quite a few accidents and bloody noses every time more than one car stopped at an intersection.

Instead, you know exactly how to analyze the situation. It doesn't matter how many combinations of cars and drivers you encounter. None of that matters, thanks to the rule.

You also do this every time you go to a store.

We have a rule that tells us, "Find the cash register and remit the currency equal to the additive amount of the items you're purchasing."

Because of this mental chunking it doesn't matter what kind of store you're going to or even if it's a type of store you've never encountered.

Without this, you might be a little confused the first time you walk into a Mark Joyner Memorabilia Store if I were to choose to open one. "Hey, I've never been to an MJ store. How does this work?"

Instead, you would see the cash register and you'd know exactly how to behave.

If you go to a stranger's house you know how to turn on the lights even if you've never been there before.

If you go to an Ethiopian restaurant for the first time you know to ask for a menu even if you've never been to one before.

If you go to a brand-new clothing store selling only pink shirts, you know to ask for the changing room if you want to try something on even if you have purchased at only the blue shirt store before.

Your brain is filled with a relatively small number of rules that use prechunking to allow you to respond to an infinite number of potential situations.

Hey . . .

What if you had a set of rules that would allow you to prechunk every single bit of business advice you ever got?

Instead of being overwhelmed by the breakneck rate at which new information is expanding . . .

Instead of being confused every time a new marketing theory is introduced . . .

What if you knew instantly whether or not something were useful?

What if you knew instantly how to categorize it for easy reference in your mind?

That tool exists, and it's called . . .

CHAPTER 5

The Great Formula

L et's start with a definition.

The Great Formula

Step 1: Create The Irresistible Offer (TIO)

Step 2: Present it to a Thirsty Crowd.

Step 3: Sell them a Second Glass.

That's it.

Every single thing you learn about marketing fits somewhere inside these three steps.

Is it really that simple?

If you look at the greatest business successes in the history of the world, you will find that nearly every one of them follows this formula to the letter.

Some got Step 1 right to a greater or lesser degree, but without exception they all excelled at Steps 2 and 3.

But you already know this to a certain extent since you've read *The Irresistible Offer*.

We'll dig a bit deeper into each step in the following chapters. In fact, we'll take a look at so many examples and permutations of this formula that you will have it mastered by the time you have read through to the end of this book.

First, let's take a look at . . .

CHAPTER 6

Why The Great Formula Works

There are three, and only three, ways to increase the revenue of any business endeavor:

1. Get your message in front of more eyeballs.

2. Get more money per eyeball.

3. Sell more products to your existing customers on the back end.

I defy you to find any way of increasing the revenue of your business that does not fall into one of these three categories.

Go on, tough guy—give it a shot.

"Improve the quality of your advertising?"

That's Category 1. Go ahead, give it another shot.

"Increase the exposure of your advertising?"

Category 1 again.

"Increase sales conversion?"

That would be Category 2.

Shall we keep going?

"Aha! I've got you now, Joyner. What about cutting costs? Where does that fit in?"

Sorry, amigo. That's Category 2 as well. If you cut the cost of running your business you're effectively earning more money per eyeball.

I'll let you work this out to its logical conclusion.

Go ahead and take out a pen and paper and see if you can find any way to increase the revenue of your business that doesn't fall into one of these three categories.

Go ahead. Try it.

Are you back?

Great. Now that you get it, here's a really important question to ask.

If these are the only three ways to increase the revenue of a business, why is it that most business owners spend about 95 percent of their time on things that *don't* fall into those three categories?

Damn good question.

If one were to take all of the actions performed in a business, isolate those actions that are making a profit, and increase the effectiveness of those actions at each step, profitability is the unavoidable result.

How do you do that?

Simple: You focus your efforts on The Great Formula.

Outside of the logistical and administrative portion of your business, The Great Formula represents every single meaningful thing you can do in your business.

Further, your logistical and administrative functions should all be *subordinate* to your work with The Great Formula.

The Great Formula works because it focuses your mind like a laser on what *works*, and forces everything else to fall by the wayside.

In the spirit of that, the rest of this book concentrates on helping you understand the nuances of The Great Formula and gives you some effective tools for applying it to your business.

After I analyze each step a little more deeply, I'll hand you over to an eclectic panel of experts I've assembled. They'll show you exactly how they've used The Great Formula to great effect.

Seeing how many different ways The Great Formula can be applied to a wide spectrum of businesses (from computer code writers to churches) should give you an inkling of just how powerful this formula is.

And it should also give you a veritable arsenal of new business ideas, and not just any ideas—meaningful ideas that fit into The Great Formula.

CHAPTER 7

The Great Formula Step 1: Create The Irresistible Offer

Since this is the sequel to a book that talked about The Irresistible Offer in depth, there is no need to rehash all of the details here.

Let's just give a quick review. . . .

The Irresistible Offer is not an "irresistible offer."

The Irresistible Offer is not a unique selling proposition (USP).

The Irresistible Offer is not a mission statement, a list of benefits, or anything else you've been taught in business school or in any other marketing book.

> **The Irresistible Offer is an identity-building offer central to a product, service, or company** where the believable return on investment is communicated so clearly and efficiently that it's immediately apparent you'd have to be a fool to pass it up.

When executed properly, The Irresistible Offer will allow you to:

- Stand out amid a blaring cacophony of marketing messages blasted at consumers all day long.
- Turbocharge your word-of-mouth efforts by programming your customers to unconsciously spread your most important marketing message from person to person like a virus.
- Sell from a position of total integrity while simultaneously beating out the majority of the marketing world that is using coercion and psychological trickery.
- Sell your customer on your products and services in three seconds or less by immediately answering the Big Four Questions:

  1. What are you trying to sell me?

  2. What is the cost?

  3. Why should I believe you?

  4. What's in it for me?

Is it all coming back to you now?

Maybe this will help. The Irresistible Offer has three equally important parts:

1. High ROI Offer.

2. Touchstone.

3. Believability.

Although I'm giving this a light treatment here, you should not give it such a light treatment in your business.

An entire book was devoted to this subject because it is the most important core function of your business. Even if you don't have The Irresistible Offer your business might do well, but you could also run your car on corn oil if you make some modifications.

The Irresistible Offer is like the high-octane jet fuel for your business that multiplies the effectiveness of everything else you do.

Don't let that prevent you from using Steps 2 and 3 of The Great Formula, though. Applying them now can give an immediate boost to your business even if you don't have The Irresistible Offer.

While The Irresistible Offer (TIO) takes time to construct and implement, you can apply Steps 2 and 3 today. In fact, I'd be surprised if by the end of this book you didn't have a full handful of ideas you can use to increase your profits the moment you put this book down.

Read on. . . .

CHAPTER 8

The Great Formula Step 2: Present It to a Thirsty Crowd

Imagine you just created the ultimate hairbrush.

When you use this hairbrush it automatically makes your hair silky-smooth.

Wind or color damage? It automatically restructures your hair back to its original healthy configuration with a single stroke.

And get this:

It will change the molecular structure of your hair in such a way that you can instantly go from curly to straight, from red to blond, from fine to thick. . . .

What's your TIO?

Heck, a product like that would make it easy. Here's one right off the top of my head:

ÜberBrush

Change your hair color,
and fix damaged hair,

with a single stroke

or 10 times your money back.

Incidentally, this is why the first part of The Irresistible Offer is a High ROI Offer. Start with a great product and the marketing becomes easy. It never ceases to amaze me—if businesses would spend as much time improving their products as they do trying to cover up mistakes, success would come much more easily.

With a product like the ÜberBrush it would be quite hard to screw up, wouldn't it?

You're very excited and you plan your big launch. A publicist you hire finds you an opportunity to give out your new product at a convention that will have more than 100,000 attendees!

You get thousands of your hairbrushes produced and you ship them off to the convention center.

You fly in the day before the launch to set up your booth. You are full of excitement. But when you enter the convention hall, your heart sinks.

You see a sign and it reads:

FIFTH ANNUAL CONVENTION OF THE TOTALLY BALD MEN OF AMERICA

That is not what I would call a Thirsty Crowd, at least not for hairbrushes.

If you were selling a hairbrush that *grew* hair, you'd have the *ultimate* Thirsty Crowd, but your brush is for people who *have* hair.

Make sense?

If you're selling horse saddles, you don't set up a tent to sell them at Oz Fest. You strike up deals with stables selling horses and have them direct mail your catalog to their customers in exchange for a cut of the profit.

If you're selling calculators, you don't go to the beach. You find a convention of mathematicians.

It doesn't matter how great your product is—if you pitch it to the wrong market you won't even make a paltry dent in your sales goals.

Imagine, however, that you find a group of people who are *thirsty* for your product.

If someone were walking through the desert and you were the only one selling water, would it be easy to make the sale?

Of course it would. In fact, your water wouldn't even have to be all that good.

Now, combine that thirst with TIO, and what do you have? Nothing short of sales fireworks, my friend.

And if the fortune you just raked in there weren't enough . . .

CHAPTER 9

The Great Formula Step 3: Sell Them a Second Glass

L et's get back to our hairbrush story.

You fire your incompetent publicist after consulting with a marketing consultant adept in The Great Formula, and the consultant helps you find your Thirsty Crowd.

You run a single infomercial in the middle of a daytime soap opera, and the results are stunning.

Knowing that 90 percent of the people glued to television sets watching daytime soaps are housewives, you hit the jackpot of Thirsty Crowds.

As you start planning your early retirement, you get a phone call from your consultant.

"I figured out a way to triple the revenue from your infomercial. Are you interested?"

Suddenly the mental picture of your retirement home turns into a castle on the beach. You can barely choke out the words, "Uh, yeah. Wow. Of course."

He then explains a little concept called the "upsell."

When people call in to purchase your hairbrush, rather than let them walk away having purchased only one, your phone staff triples your business with a single question:

"Would you like to add on any additional brushes at 50 percent off for your mother, your daughter, or any of your friends?"

Fifty percent off? Wow, what a bargain! The purchaser then has an excited conversation with your phone staff about any upcoming birthdays or weddings and ends up purchasing a whopping five more brushes before she hangs up.

How could she resist? At 50 percent off she'd be crazy to pass that up.

And you would be crazy not to incorporate this or one of the many Second Glass tactics available to your business.

See how easy it is?

It's an insider's secret that none of the great fortunes of the world have been built on the first glass. They were all built by selling a Second Glass of *something*.

Prepare to have your mind expanded as you witness some rather unexpected ways this concept has been applied by real-world business owners in the trenches. The possibilities are just as staggering as the implications.

Before I tell you some of these stories, let's create a foundation of skills upon which you can build. . . .

CHAPTER 10

In Search of the Thirsty Crowd

Thirsty Crowds are everywhere if you know *how* to look.

When most people think of getting their marketing message in front of an audience, they think of classic advertising: television, radio, newspapers, magazines. . . .

Yes, used properly the classic media can give you direct access to huge Thirsty Crowds. This is only one of four ways you can find Thirsty Crowds, though.

There are infinite ways to find a Thirsty Crowd, and some of them are actually quite cheap or even free.

Yes, there are infinite methods, but all of the ones I have seen fall into what I call . . .

The Four Strategies for Capturing Thirsty Crowds

1. Pay for access to a crowd.

2. Speculate for access to a crowd.

3. Manifest a crowd from thin air.

4. Find lost crowds.

Let's take a look at each one in detail.

PAY FOR ACCESS TO A CROWD

We're talking about the standard classic stuff here.

You find a magazine whose readership is precisely your Thirsty Crowd. You then purchase ad space in the magazine.

Obviously, an ad in the properly targeted medium will greatly outpull an ad in the wrong place. Again, you don't advertise hairbrushes to bald men (unless your magic brush *grows* hair).

Not only can you purchase advertising in classic media, but you can also purchase access to crowds created by businesses that sell to your market. In fact, you're far more likely to find the most responsive Thirsty Crowds strike that way than in the classic media.

Think about it. Who do you think is more likely to purchase your worms? A viewer of a television show on fishing or someone who has purchased a fishing pole?

So, how does this work? Well, many businesses know that a great way to increase revenue is to rent access to their lists (an interesting alternative Second Glass tactic). Through list brokers you can find thousands upon thousands of businesses willing to rent their lists to you for a fairly reasonable fee.

Anyway, this is just scratching the surface. I'll let my guest experts fill you in on some crazy possibilities you may have never imagined later on.

SPECULATE FOR ACCESS TO A CROWD

Don't feel like paying for access?

No problem. You don't have to.

Many people who have access to Thirsty Crowds will grant you access on spec.

Here's how it works. Let's say you sell some rather high-end shampoo targeted to rich people who want to look good no matter the cost.

You find a boutique salon with an upper-class clientele and you approach the owner.

"Let me put my shampoo in your salon at no cost to you. Whenever you sell a bottle, keep 50 percent and don't pay me a dime unless you make a sale."

Easy as pie—you both grab money that was "sitting on the table" with very little additional effort.

Later on, after the salon has sold a few bottles, you approach the owner and suggest, "Say, what if you sent out a letter to all of your clients offering my shampoo at a discount? I'll even pay for the cost of the printing and mailing. I'll give you 50 percent of the purchase price for every bottle we sell."

For a very low cost and minimal risk you just gained access to an extremely Thirsty Crowd.

Want to lower the risk even more? Wait until the salon's next planned mailing and ask them to insert your ad with the existing mailing. Heck—you just got the cost down to whatever Kinko's charges you for duplication.

The possibilities here are endless. In fact, there have been periods in my business life when almost all of my profits were earned using this strategy.

MANIFEST A CROWD FROM THIN AIR

Every time you encounter potential customers, even if they don't buy, you should always capture their contact information and get permission to send them offers in the future.

If browsers walk into your store, get them on your mailing list.

If visitors come to your web site, ask them to sign up for your e-mail newsletter.

If you're doing a trade show and someone walks up to your booth, capture the person's contact info.

Every little bit of contact you have with a potential customer is a chance to slowly build your own Thirsty Crowd. You'll observe some unexpected examples of this shortly.

Of course, your best Thirsty Crowd is your list of existing customers, and that's why selling the Second Glass is so easy; but more on that soon . . .

FIND LOST CROWDS

Sometimes Thirsty Crowds are just *there*, and all you have to do is sneak in your marketing message.

On the Internet, there are millions of discussion communities and almost certainly you'll find some in your niche. Get yourself known there by helping out the members, and you'll build a loyal following. Don't be afraid to give away samples generously. Heck, some of the community members might even advertise your product on your behalf simply because they are so ecstatic with the service you've provided.

Here's another approach. . . .

If you go to a nightclub in Miami, New York, or Los Angeles, you can't leave the place at closing time without getting accosted by promoters from competitive clubs handing you passes to their venues.

This one is bordering on crowd hijacking, which I'd avoid like the plague if I were you, but it should open up your mind to possibilities.

Lost Thirsty Crowds are roaming the world just waiting for you to find them.

In the chapters to follow you'll discover some rather unexpected ways to apply these methods.

CHAPTER 11

Second Glass Tactics

In *The Irresistible Offer* I gave a pretty comprehensive look at Second Glass delivery methods and even some "Second Glass recipes."

Of equal importance is the section on "How to Keep the Door Open."

I would highly recommend referring back to that section time and time again. Anytime you're short of marketing ideas, that section should get your creative juices flowing.

We'll give you some real-world examples shortly (some of them will have you gushing in admiration at the ingenuity of these cunning entrepreneurs), but let's give a quick recap first of . . .

The Four Second-Glass Delivery Methods

1. The upsell
2. The cross-sell
3. The follow-up
4. The continuity

Just as there are limitless ways to find Thirsty Crowds, there are limitless ways to deliver a Second Glass. Most, but not all, of the Second Glass recipes in existence fit into one of these four categories.

Let's give a quick recap of the four methods.

THE UPSELL

If you're selling them a small version of a product, they may very well be interested in a large version. If they're buying "light," why not offer them "deluxe" instead?

If the offer for the supersized version of your product is just as irresistible as the original product, it shouldn't be overly difficult to turn a $10 sale into a $100 sale.

Just don't abuse this approach. If you upsell someone crap—products or services that don't offer a higher ROI for the money they're laying out—they're gone forever. All efforts to regain your credibility will be in vain.

THE CROSS-SELL

If you're selling someone a car, wouldn't the buyer also be interested in a good sound system? If you are a dentist and you perform teeth cleaning, wouldn't the same customer possibly be interested in teeth whitening?

The approach obviously needs to be used carefully here, lest you insult your customer. "Oh, so you think my teeth are ugly?" Overly aggressive or insulting upsells are customer-repellent. They might produce an initial sale if the snake doing the pushing is clever, but the customer will associate so much pain with the process that he will avoid coming back. A dentist stacking emotional pain onto the physical pain built into the office visit is sure to leave a lasting impression on the customer!

Home electronics stores have become masters of the cross-sell. If you're shelling out the money for a big-screen television, they can easily convince you that, once you've made that initial investment, you ought to spend a little more to get the right cables and other accessories to ensure a perfect picture.

Such cross-sell offers can increase your profit per sale dramatically.

Think about it. If you make 1,000 sales a month and add just $1 in profit on accessories and add-ons for each sale, that's an extra $12,000 in profit per year.

If the cross-sells are legitimately helping the customer to get a better result, he won't feel like you pitched him. He'll feel like you helped him! There's a huge difference. Helping customers not only renders more sales, but also stimulates positive word of mouth. (More on that shortly . . .)

THE FOLLOW-UP

The two methods mentioned can be used immediately at the point of sale.

Just make sure you do your cross-sells and upsells *after* the first sale is consummated. If you overload your customers with options before the deal is sealed, you may just confuse them right out the door. Have you ever put two bones in front of a dog? What does he do? He is so confused that he doesn't bury either of them. He simply can't commit because he has too many options. Humans, whether we care to admit it or not, are just as easily confused.

Keep it simple.

The follow-up sale is one that occurs at *any* time thereafter.

It may be a day later. It may be a year later.

See "How to Keep the Door Open" in *The Irresistible Offer* for some useful tools.

THE CONTINUITY

Some products just lend themselves to a natural Second Glass. For example, a subscription to a monthly magazine is, in itself, a Second, a Third, a Fourth, and so on.

"Continuity" products are those that are offered to the customer on a regular basis. It's, in essence, built-in, guaranteed repeat sales.

You may not have heard the name Guthy-Renker, but you've no doubt seen their infomercials. They're one of the world's leading television infomercial marketers. An insider there told me that they no longer even consider taking on new products that aren't continuity-based.

For example, Guthy Renker sells a superb skin-care line that comes with a discount for automatic monthly refills. The product works very well—it has a high ROI ("You invest some money, we give you beautiful skin")—and therefore people are happily paying for it month after month. The company gets its customers to commit to monthly payments to keep them on board. It's a bit aggressive, but if you're offering a product that works and is reasonably priced, then continuity is doable and leads to perpetual profits.

Overdeliver on every helping and you'll sell more and more. Here are a few ideas for keeping your customer coming back for more that may spark your imagination.

CHAPTER 12

The Great Formula in History

The following examples demonstrate a small sampling of the many companies that have amassed massive fortunes using The Great Formula.

Some of these companies have followed the formula a little more closely than others. Armed now with what you know, let's see if you could improve on the success of these companies using your knowledge of The Irresistible Offer and The Great Formula.

HOLIDAY INN

Have you ever taken a road trip?

You know—when you get in your car with your family, drive across country, and just "see the world"? If you have, you've probably noticed that the quality of the accommodations you get along the way (unless you're paying for five-star service at every stop) can vary dramatically.

Some of the motels you stop at are clean and well-kept, while others look like they've come straight out of a B-grade horror movie.

In 1951 Kemmons Wilson went on a road trip with his family and had much the same experience you might get today when you play "motel roulette." To make matters worse, most motels back then were charging an extra $2 a head for children. The going rate was $8 to $10 a night, so having his five kids in tow was doubling Wilson's costs.

His frustration inspired him to open up his own franchise of motorhotels, and exactly one year later the first Holiday Inn was born.

The Thirsty Crowd: Vacationing Families

Back then there were generally two classes of accommodation in the United States.

You had your upscale, expensive hotels, primarily found in urban areas. Then you had your mom-and-pop motels scattered along the highways everywhere, and although these were more affordable, the quality tended to be hit-or-miss.

Wilson had a vision of creating something in between, something that did not exist at the time.

According to *Fortune Magazine*, "Travelers would receive a clean room, a comfortable bed, an on-site restaurant, lounge, swimming pool, laundry, free ice machines—and oh, yes, kids would stay free if they slept in the same room as their parents."

Any family that had survived the motel potluck of a road trip was certainly thirsty for what he was offering.

The Irresistible Offer

High ROI Offer

Clean, reliable rooms, at a good rate.

Touchstone

Holiday Inn has run several, starting with "The best surprise is no surprise." Then it was "Kids stay free." And since that is no longer remarkable, it's now "Kids eat free."

And just to prove that no one gets it right all the time, the rather lackluster "You're No. 1" appeared in 1968. (See the following page.)

Believability

All you had to do was look at the Holiday Inn and you could see for yourself that it delivered. (It's easy to sell a product where customers can see the quality with their own eyes.)

The Second Glass

This is where Holiday Inns cleaned up. On-site, they had restaurants and vending machines that added immediate Second Glass earnings, but where they really hit home runs was in repeat business.

In 1965 Holiday Inn revolutionized the hotel industry with the "Holidex" computer system—then the world's largest civilian computer network. Two IBM mainframes in Memphis,

Tennessee, connected every Holiday Inn to a centralized reservation system.

The clerk at one Holiday Inn could book a traveling family into another Holiday Inn a day away.

Of course the families loved it because they had "no surprises" at their next stop, and Holiday Inn raked in profits as a result.

According to *USA Today*, Wilson was quoted as saying, "It gave us a huge edge over our competitors, and from that day on, it wasn't a matter of selling franchises. It was a matter of taking orders for them."

GILLETTE SAFETY RAZOR

Here's another legendary business created by a dissatisfied traveler.

Today we take the disposable safety razor blade for granted. Anyone caught shaving with a straight razor these days might even be considered a little bit eccentric. There are some out there who claim the straight razor gives the closest shave you can get, but I haven't been able to get it to work. Back to my disposable blades for me.

Back in 1895, however, there weren't many alternatives. The cutthroat straight razor was the weapon of choice of most men, but it was dangerous and required a lot of maintenance.

King Gillette (that was his name; he wasn't the king of anything—except razors later in life) used to wake up every morning to a shave from his "Star Safety Razor." As a traveling salesman, Gillette spent many of his days on the road and often shaved in the lavatory of a moving train. The safety razor was the only alternative to the straight razor at the time. Essentially it was a wedge-shaped blade attached to a handle at 90 degrees. This made it easier to use and not nearly as dangerous as the standard straight razor, but Gillette was frustrated to find that he was still forced to strop the blade frequently to keep it sharp.

In a flash of inspiration he imagined a blade that would never need sharpening. Once it lost its edge, you'd simply throw it away and install a new one in the holder.

He teamed up with an MIT engineer named William Emory Nickerson, and the disposable blade was born.

The Thirsty Crowd

Gillette's frustration was rather common back then, and what a market size! Almost all men in the industrialized world shaved every single day.

In 1915, he went on to create the first "lady razor" and expanded his market to "every single person in the industrialized world with unwanted body hair."

The Irresistible Offer

High ROI Offer

For a reasonable fee, you'd get a packet of throwaway blades that lasted 20 to 40 days, wouldn't cut your skin, and never needed sharpening. The users genuinely saved time and money and worry.

Touchstone

The company has run several over the years as times changed, ranging from the lackluster "We have a new razor" to the more

No. 775,134.

PATENTED NOV. 15, 1904.

K. C. GILLETTE.
RAZOR.
APPLICATION FILED DEC. 3, 1901.

NO MODEL.

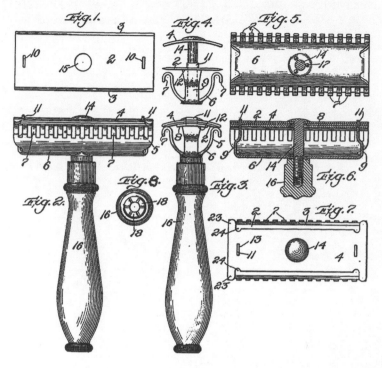

Witnesses:
Ruby M. Banfield.
Margaret A. Daniher.

By

Inventor:
King C. Gillette,

E. A. Chadwick,
Attorney.

55

inspired "'The Gillette' saves 15 days' time each year," "10 extra blades, 20 sharp edges, good for a year, 50 cents," and "No stropping. No honing."

The Gillette Company never seemed to hit on a brand identity with its Touchstones, and even today is struggling with such dull touchstones as "The best a man can get." Perhaps the company's excellence in the other aspects of The Great Formula, combined with its early market dominance and innovations, has allowed it to succeed despite uninspiring Touchstones.

Believability

An early shrewd move included testimonials from famous baseball players like Hall of Famer Honus Wagner.

The Second Glass

Disposable razors, we know now, are a classic Second Glass offering. Heck, disposable *anything* makes for a great Second Glass (albeit a potentially terrible thing for the environment unless it's biodegradable).

Gillette learned during his days working at Crown Cork bottle caps that disposable items could be a gold mine. He was given the great advice at that time to just "invent something people use and throw away," according to *Fortune Magazine*.

Gillette was so excited about this proposition that he said, "The greatest feature of the business is the almost endless chain of blade consumption, each razor paying tribute to the company as long as the user lives."

He knew that the real value of his company was found in the "lifetime value" of his customers, but was faced with the dilemma of how to get people to come up with the pricey $5 needed to purchase his razor to which the disposable blades

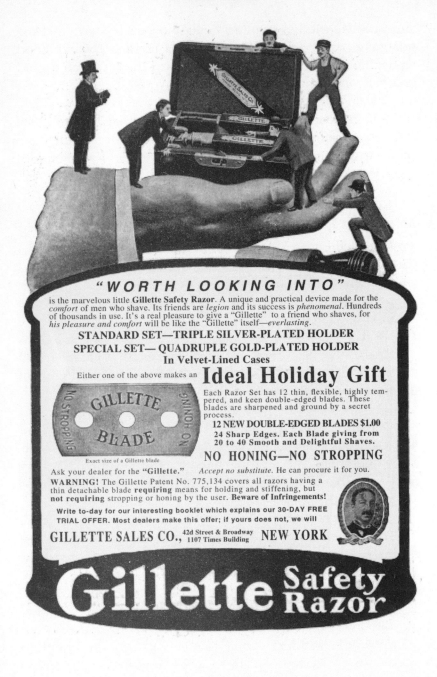

attached. He tried everything to convince consumers that the relatively costly razor (which "lasted a lifetime") was a good value. Then, at the onset of World War I, he hit upon a bold and risky idea on how to gain new converts.

Gillette proposed to give a razor to every soldier as he entered the military. He knew that there would be a tremendous up-front cost in doing this, but believed the gain in new lifetime customers would ultimately outweigh the expense.

His company execs were excited by this idea and took it a step further. Instead of giving one razor away to every soldier, they decided on the philanthropic move of selling their blades and razors to the government at cost. The government agreed, and Gillette designed a special metal-case shaving kit for the infantryman and packaged it with the touchstone "Every man in khaki ought to have one."

By the end of the war, the government had purchased 3.5 million razors and 32 million blades. Since Gillette was doing this at cost, what was the upside?

Well, the young servicemen came home as converts to the new blades, so the military monopoly, while not profitable in itself, ended up seeding future profits. Furthermore, the company was able to develop a massive infrastructure with virtually zero risk.

The tremendous success from the company's World War I efforts spurred what former Gillette CEO Joseph Sprang called "the give-away years." They gave away razors with everything they could think of from chewing gum to pocket knives and canned meat.

In 1953 Gillette broadened its Second Glass offerings even

further. The company launched offerings for canned shaving foam, and its profits exploded.

Today Gillette has gone the way of many large companies, selling so many things (from batteries to toothbrushes) that it's hard to pin down a solid identity for it. However, Gillette used The Great Formula to the letter to get to that point.

Gillette is now widely recognized as one of the 10 most valuable brands in the world (among greats like Coca-Cola).

AMAZON.COM

In 1994 Wall Street executive Jeff Bezos noticed that Internet usage was growing at the staggering rate of 2,300 percent every year.

He examined the mail-order business world searching for a niche that would benefit from electronic cataloging. There was one niche ripe for the plucking that no one else seemed to recognize at the time: books. No comprehensive sales catalog existed for books at the time, and for obvious reasons. A warehouse that contained every book in existence would be far too big to be profitable.

So, Bezos started Cadabra in his home (named after the word abracadabra) using just three Sun workstations on a table in his living room (the table was made out of a $60 door from Home Depot). Since the major book wholesalers already had electronic inventories of their books, all he needed to do was provide one central Internet location to host the combined inventory.

Bezos found that whenever he told people about Cadabra they tended to confuse the name with "cadaver," so he

60

changed it to Amazon, after the earth's longest river. He opened his doors in July 1995 and by September was taking in $20,000 in orders per week.

Amazon.com is now the largest bookstore in the world and one of the greatest business success stories in history.

The Irresistible Offer

High ROI Offer

Amazon offered, at the time, the only Internet location with such a wide selection of books. You'd get the same books you could buy at a bookstore, and save time by browsing an electronic database from the comfort of your home. Add to that a significant savings in price as well as fast delivery, and you have the recipe for some very happy customers.

According to *Wired*, Bezos summed it up very astutely: "If your brand is based exclusively on price, you're in a fragile position, but if your brand is about great prices and great service and great selection, that is a much better position."

Touchstone

Amazon has outgrown its touchstone as "The earth's biggest bookstore," since it now sells quite a few things besides books, but the touchstone served Amazon long enough to give the company a clearly dominant position in the marketplace.

Believability

With all of the e-buzz going on back in 1995, Amazon lucked out with a tremendous amount of free publicity. The sheer buzzworthiness of being the first made Amazon the talk of the press, and you can't find a better credibility-building tool than

61

that. If the press is talking about them, of course they're legitimate—what's not to believe?

The Thirsty Crowd

The book market was already there. Billions of dollars' worth of books were being sold every year world-wide long before Amazon came onto the scene. It goes to show that any existing market can be hijacked if you simply outclass your competition with The Irresistible Offer—especially if your High ROI Offer is clearly superior.

Brand loyalty will get you only so far when your competitor is clearly taking better care of your customers—especially if they're getting free international publicity every day.

Customers may love you, but only as long as you're holding up your end of the bargain.

Amazon expanded its access to Thirsty Crowds by letting other people find them. The company invented "affiliate marketing" whereby people recommending their products would be rewarded with a small commission every time the recommendation resulted in a sale.

By 2003 Amazon had more than a million of these freelancing sales "associates" generating Thirsty Crowd hunting across the globe. Amazon associates are now responsible for about 40 percent of Amazon's sales.

The Second Glass

Amazon.com may be the hands-down Second Glass master.

The company follows up with consumers by sending out newsletters and product recommendations.

It has instant upsells and cross-sells integrated seamlessly into its sales process.

And much of the time the power of Amazon's "top of mind" branding brings customers back without any additional prompting.

CHARLES ATLAS: "THE SAND-IN-THE-FACE BOY BECOMES 'THE WORLD'S MOST PERFECTLY DEVELOPED MAN'"

One of the staples of pulp fiction novels and comic books in the early twentieth century was the classic image of a "97-pound weakling" getting "sand kicked in his face" and having his girl stolen away by a brawny life guard.

It is reported that this "Charles Atlas" story is based on an actual event that happened to Atlas (then known as Angelo Charles Siciliano) on Coney Island, New York, when he was a teen. Apparently a muscular lifeguard really did kick sand in his face and his less-than-impressed date walked off.

Not long after, Atlas was watching large cats exercising in the Brooklyn Zoo, and realized that these powerful animals kept themselves fit simply by working one muscle against another. The Coney Island incident had already inspired Atlas to join the local YMCA gym, but he now discarded his weights and developed a new form of muscular exercises called "dynamic tension." Using these isometric techniques, Atlas succeeded in transforming himself from a scrawny young man into a spectacularly sculpted hulk. It is reported that he then spotted a statue of the Ancient Greek figure Atlas and decided to take on the name, and the legend was born. (Atlas was a mighty Titan who, as punishment for battling against Zeus, ruler of the gods, was forced to bear the heavens on his back.)

The Irresistible Offer

High ROI Offer

Charles Atlas Ltd. delivered an exercise program that genuinely did have a positive effect on the physiques of those who used it.

Touchstone

All you had to do was "gamble a stamp" and they'd send you a free book titled *Everlasting Health and Strength* that showed you how to turn into a buff husky Adonis without the need for weights.

Believability

Atlas famously won the title of "The World's Most Perfectly Developed Man" in a Madison Square Garden bodybuilding competition and immediately leveraged his success to tout the benefits of his dynamic tension program.

The Thirsty Crowd

In 1928 Atlas teamed up with an advertising executive by the name of Charles P. Roman who, after hearing Atlas's story, recognized that any young man who has been bullied surely secretly dreams of beating the crap out of the bully and winning the girl. Roman also observed that young men typically read pulp fiction and comic books and so found easy access to a crowd extremely thirsty from emotional bruising. They developed a short comic strip called "Mac's Story" or "The insult that made a man out of Mac," which they based on Atlas's Coney Island experience, and featured this enormously popular cartoon in comics and newspapers.

The Second Glass

Charles Atlas Ltd. hooked customers with a free book after "gambling a stamp" (I love that phrase) and then upsold them on a yearlong course that promised results in "7 days."

Today Charles Atlas Ltd. has turned to manufacturing vitamin supplements and exercise gear.

The Atlas book, which continues in popularity, has been translated into seven languages. The company's ads were a staple of the pulp press for decades.

TIN LIZZIE

Henry Ford incorporated the Ford Motor Company in 1903 at a time when automobiles were considered luxury playthings and enjoyed by only the very wealthy.

Ford famously proclaimed that one day he would "build a car for the great multitude," and that he did. The Model T (lovingly known as the "Tin Lizzie") was released in 1908; it sold for $950, one-third the price of other motorcars at the time.

Ford went on to revolutionize the manufacturing industry with the invention of the assembly line. This cut the production time for a Model T from 12 hours to 93 minutes.

He then did a number of other radical things that dramatically increased production. He paid his employees $5 an hour, nearly double the wages paid by his competitors, and cut their workday down to eight hours so he could run three shifts a day.

In 1914, Ford produced 308,162 cars—more than all of the other 299 existing car manufacturers combined. And by 1927, Ford's innovative manufacturing techniques enabled the automaker to crank out a new car every 24 seconds.

The Model T was manufactured for 19 years, and by the end of its production 15,500,000 Model Ts had been sold in the United States alone.

The Irresistible Offer

High ROI Offer

The average person could now travel 10 times faster in a Model T than with most alternative forms of personal transportation. It wasn't the fastest or most beautiful machine on the road, but it was cheap and reliable.

Touchstone

Own an automobile for one-third the price.

Believability

Again the power of the press gives a wonderful gift to a great innovator. If you're that buzzworthy, you'll get a tremendous amount of natural publicity and that will give you an unprecedented seal of approval.

It's interesting to note that by 1914 the Model T was selling so well that Ford dropped most of its national ads—what was the need? By 1917 the automaker had halted advertising altogether. It did not advertise again until 1923, when Ford began to target women drivers and young men eager for their first car.

The Thirsty Crowd

Again we have an example of a universally appealing product, the Thirsty Crowd for which is not hard to find. The great multitude was hungry for a faster way to get from A to B. How long do you think it would take "personal jet packs" to find a Thirsty Crowd today? You have to understand that owning a car back then was almost equivalent to that.

The Second Glass

One look at Ford's web site today will show you a wide range of Second Glass offerings. The obvious is a new replacement car when the one you own wears out (or another Ford when you want to buy one for additional members of your family), but the company doesn't stop there.

The automaker offers vehicle financing services, replacement parts, mechanical services, vehicle insurance, and various brand-related accessories and merchandise. It also offers the lucrative Ford Extended Service Plan, which is an extension of the manufacturer warranty for Ford, Lincoln, and Mercury cars.

EDMONDS BAKING POWDER AND COOKBOOK

In 1879, a 20-year-old Kiwi (New Zealander) grocer named Thomas J. Edmonds noticed that his customers frequently complained about the quality of baking powder available at the time.

Customers would come into his shop lamenting that their cakes and scones had failed to rise.

In response, Edmonds developed his own baking powder that he guaranteed would rise every time, and an icon was born.

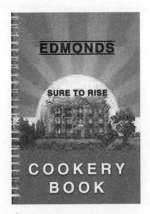

In 1907, he released a cookbook that contained 50 pages of tried-and-true recipes and cookery tips. Each recipe featured one or more of Edmonds' own products. The *Edmonds Cookery Book* became the most successful cookbook in the history of the country. In fact, it remains today the biggest-selling book ever published in New Zealand and it's now considered standard to give a copy of the "good ol' Edmonds" to young people when they move out of the family home and into their first apartment. You can scarcely find a grocery store in the country that doesn't carry a copy in the bakery goods aisle—and it is likely to be the only cookbook you'll see there.

Anna Stillaman, my stellar personal assistant, is a New Zealander, and she told this story to demonstrate how intrinsically interwoven the book has become with the country's culture. Kiwis are known to hop over to the baking goods aisle and flip through the *Edmonds Cookery Book* if they are short on ideas for dinner.

The Irresistible Offer

High ROI Offer

Edmonds promised a baking powder that would rise every time, and it worked. There was a tremendous amount of pressure on Kiwi women back then to be culinary successes, so the offer was hard to resist.

Touchstone

"Sure to Rise."

Believability

I suppose you don't need much when you claim to do something everyone wants. That's enough to get people to at least try it and then word of mouth will take care of the rest.

Second Glass

Now here is a work of pure genius.

Edmonds offered the *Edmonds Cookery Book*, a natural Second Glass. But it didn't stop there. Over time, the company introduced new cooking products, and the trusted recipes in the faithful cookbook were updated to incorporate all the latest Edmonds offerings, spurring further sales of both the cookbook and the products.

ESTÉE LAUDER

Estée Lauder got her start in the 1930s by selling face creams developed by her chemist uncle, John Schotz, in a makeshift laboratory behind the family house.

Lauder was eager to create an empire of her own, however, and starting experimenting with her own mixtures in her kitchen. She hit on some great formulas and began shopping them to boutique stores at high prices. She had such a passion for her work that she would go to Saks Fifth Avenue herself and rub the creams on the hands of women passing by, confident that the product would sell itself. She was right. The creams were an instant hit with most of the women who tried them.

You could even find her on Fifth Avenue stopping women on the street to invite them to sample her cream. Her passion was legendary, and so was the success of her business; various Estée Lauder products are now being sold in every major department store.

The Irresistible Offer

High ROI Offer

The products truly were superior, actually improving the appearance and feel of the skin on contact.

Touchstone

Her touchstone was not so much verbal as kinesthetic. Her sales process centered around the offer of free samples and testing in stores. Once customers tried the product, they were hooked.

Later, she developed a brilliant verbal touchstone: "A free gift with every purchase."

Believability

Lauder shrewdly vied for the approval of movie stars and royalty—people whom ordinary folk admired and looked up to. She understood that the endorsement of the rich and beautiful would give her products added believability for their high quality and value. Princess Grace of Monaco was quoted as saying about Lauder, "I don't know her very well, but she keeps sending all these things."

The high prices of Lauder's products were an additional believability factor. In postwar Europe, premium pricing was uncommon and manufacturers tended to steer toward the lower end of the market; Lauder, however, cunningly and accurately predicted a longing for small luxuries, and face cream was definitely a luxury rather than a necessity. Her predictions were spot on, and people associated the high prices of her products with superior quality.

The Thirsty Crowd

Lauder worked hard to get placement of her products in top-end perfumeries, department stores, and specialty retailers. A Thirsty Crowd was ready and waiting, and all she had to do was piggyback on it.

The Second Glass

Her "free gift with every purchase" touchstone created an endless stream of Second Glass opportunities. Every time you purchase an Estée Lauder product, you receive a kinesthetic ad for another in the form of a "free gift."

That's fiendishly effective marketing.

TABLE FOR SIX

The current rules of dating have made things tough for singles trying to find a date. Marketers are doing a tremendous job of keeping us all whipped up in a sexual frenzy, but it's still socially unacceptable in much of the United States for women to be as sexually active as men.

Table for Six offers a welcome alternative. For an annual fee they will connect you with a group of six people (three men and three women) based on your age and interests for an upscale night out on the town or an "adventure."

The Irresistible Offer
High ROI Offer

Plenty of introductions without the stress for a reasonable fee. No awkward phone calls. No awkward silences on unsuccessful dates.

Touchstone

"We match three single men and three single women according to similar ages, interests, and lifestyles and arrange for them to dine together at upscale restaurants."

Believability

They include plenty of testimonials and social proof in their advertising. There is also a huge potential for improved believability through word of mouth as friends tell friends about their adventures.

The Thirsty Crowd

Table for Six advertises in hip San Francisco Bay Area publications where a dating-hungry readership is likely to be found.

The Second Glass

They have arrangements with fine restaurants and tour companies in the area that will gladly pay a fee for the easy business.

CHAPTER 13

Mad Scientists Using The Great Formula

There is an underground in the worlds of direct marketing and Internet marketing responsible for a tremendous amount of innovation each year, and they scarcely get the credit they deserve.

This chapter includes stories, articles, and case studies from these Mad Scientists explaining some innovative and sometimes shocking ways they use different aspects of The Great Formula to boost their profits.

Some of the contributors (like Joe Sugarman of JS&A and BluBlocker fame) started out as small-time entrepreneurs/innovators but went on to become business icons. Others are little known outside of the underground circles, but are innovating their way into job-free livings.

I selected the Mad Scientists to give a wide range of people from a wide range of industries and varying skill levels.

The important thing to note here is that each article demonstrates that The Great Formula can be applied to any business, in any industry. It doesn't matter if you have $1,000,000 in start-up capital or you're financing your business start-up with a credit card—The Great Formula will dramatically increase your profits every single time.

I asked each contributor the following questions:

- What are the various ways people can identify and address crowds thirsty for their product?
- What are some cool ways you've done so in the past?
- What are the various ways people can offer a Second Glass to their customers (after the initial sale—the back end, essentially)?
- What are some cool ways you've done so in the past?

Some (like Andrew Fox) answered the questions directly. Some (like Gary Halbert) asked me to reprint for you some of their lost writings that illustrate their use of The Great Formula beautifully. Others (like Dr. Joe Vitale) provided stories that illustrate the point.

Each entry has its own unique value, and I urge you to pour through them all like a detective looking for clues.

Picasso Tile Illusion

Joe Sugarman

Joseph Sugarman a marketing legend, and chairman of JS&A Group, Inc.; BluBlocker Corporation; and DelStar Publishing—all based in Las Vegas, Nevada. He was raised in the Chicago area and in 1962, following three and a half years at the electrical engineering college of the University of Miami, he was drafted into the U.S. Army. He spent more than three years in Germany serving with the Army Intelligence Service and later with the CIA. Upon returning home, Joe formed a company to market Austrian ski lifts in the United States. Then in 1971, he formed a company to market the world's first pocket calculator through direct marketing (all from the basement of his home in Northbrook, Illinois). This company, JS&A Group, Inc., quickly grew to become America's largest single source of space-age products, and throughout the 1970s Joe introduced dozens of new innovations and electronic concepts, including the digital watch, cordless telephones, and computers. In 1973, JS&A Group became the first company in the United States to use the 800 WATS line service to take credit card orders over the telephone—this was something that direct marketers had never done before. Joe was selected as the Direct Marketing Man of the Year in 1979.

In 1990—five books and numerous marketing seminars later— Joe decided to focus all his energy on his line of BluBlocker sunglasses. These he sold in direct mailings, mail order ads, and catalogs, and on television through infomercials, TV spots, and QVC, the home shopping channel. He was one of the early pioneers in this direct marketing segment, having entered the field in 1987, and over 7 million pairs of BluBlocker sunglasses have since been sold through his infomercials and over 20 million pairs worldwide! In 1991, Joe won the prestigious Maxwell Sackheim award for his creative career contributions to direct marketing.

If all that wasn't enough, Joe is also a professional photographer, graphic designer, pilot, scuba diver, and public speaker. From 2000 to

2005, *he was the editor and publisher of the* Maui Weekly—*one of the fastest-growing newspapers in Hawaii—which he has recently sold to a West Virginia newspaper chain.*

To find out more about Joe Sugarman, you can visit this web site: www.BluBlocker.com

Here's an idea that worked so incredibly well that I'm surprised nobody has used it since I did in 1976.

I met somebody who was the licensing agent for Pablo Picasso. The art of Picasso, who had died in 1973, was so popular that his licensing firm was able to license everything from bedsheets to many household items—all with his images.

I got to know the licensing agent well. And one day he approached me and made a suggestion. Why not put Picasso's images on six 6″ × 6″ tiles? It had never been done before, and besides, it would be an authentic limited edition by Picasso and licensed by the Picasso family estate.

The idea appealed to me but primarily because I thought I'd have a little fun with it. First, I realized that to simply sell a limited quantity of a piece of art on a tile was okay, but I wanted to develop a business from this with ongoing sales.

I also realized that I didn't have a mailing list of strong prospects to whom I could mail the offer. And I knew that it took years to develop a strong list, anyway. And since the tile was a new art form, it might encounter buyer's resistance from the public.

I saw the marketing challenge as multifaceted. First I needed to somehow build a mailing list. Second, I had to establish a strong value for an art form that nobody had heard of with an artist who was world famous; and finally I had to do it rather quickly. I didn't want to wait years to establish a company. So here's what I did.

I took out a full-page ad in the *Wall Street Journal* offering a limited edition set of six tiles at a very reasonable price—$7 per tile. In addition, I explained that the price and the offer were limited since we had only 1,250 sets to sell and that we were not making any money from it. In fact, I showed the cost to make the tiles and the cost of the ad in the *Journal*, indicating that we were not making a penny from it. I also explained that we would surely be oversold and that we would use a "random selection process" to select the future owners of the tiles. In short, we would let our computer randomly generate who our customers would be. The ones who were not selected we would advise that the series wouldn't be available to them.

The ad ran and it was a huge success. Not only did we sell all 1,250 tile sets, but we received a total of 8,000 requests, most of which we had to turn down.

Presto! Overnight, we had a large, hot mailing list—a list that consisted of customers who were rejected and denied the opportunity of buying from me. In addition, we took the focus away from the unusual nature of the art form. It didn't matter if it was a tile or a canvas, as it was the hot nature of the limited availability of a hot collectible that was more important. And finally, we had 8,000 people who would love to buy our next offering whom we could reach by mail (thus avoiding the high cost of advertising in the *Wall Street Journal*) and of course we could earn a nice profit. And that is exactly what we did, following up with a series of Picasso tiles.

Our first mailing generated a 65.8 percent response rate—one of the highest in my career and one of the biggest responses I've ever heard of by anybody else. Typically if you received a 2 percent response that was considered good.

The subsequent promotions did very well, and with a strong base of 8,000 names we were able to build a nice business for the next few years.

Deny somebody something, create a mailing list of rejected customers, offer them something in the future, and sit back and count the profits. Not a bad way to generate a nice little business, let alone a nice income.

Two Excerpts from the Boron Letters

Gary Halbert

Gary Halbert started his direct marketing career by writing a 361-word one-page letter to sell a family crest product. Soon after that letter was mailed, it was grossing the equivalent (in today's money) of one-third of one million dollars per day. That letter (with modifications) was mailed for more than 30 years.

Gary's clients have included Ron LeGrand, Robert Allen, Mark Victor Hansen, Ernest and Tova Borgnine, Vikki LaMatta, Phillips Publishing, CASI Publishing, Agora Financial, and many others too numerous to mention.

One of the letters Gary wrote for Phillips Publishing used a penny attached to the first page of the sales letter as a grabber. Phillips Publishing actually had the Denver Mint produce millions of extra pennies in order to send that letter to all of the mailing lists. Even with that added expense, Gary's sales letter produced an enormous profit for Phillips Publishing.

In 1984 Gary's direct response business had a bit of a brush with the law and he spent a year in Boron State Penitentiary. He used that time to write a series of letters to his son Bond in which he passes on wisdom about life, family, and direct marketing. Gary has generously allowed me to include two of those very personal letters to his son here.

Currently, Gary publishes the most widely read marketing newsletter in the world.

You can learn more about Gary Halbert at his exceptional web site at www.TheGaryHalbertLetter.com.

Sunday, 10:16 A.M.
June 17, 1984

Dear Bond,

No messing around. I'm going to dive right back into the subject of becoming a "student of markets."

As you know, once in a while I give a class on copywriting and/or selling by mail. One of the questions I like to ask my students is: "If you and I both owned a hamburger stand and we were in a contest to see who would sell the most hamburgers, what advantages would you most like to have on your side?"

The answers vary. Some people say they would like to have the advantage of having superior meat from which to make their hamburgers. Others say they want sesame seed buns. Others mention location. Someone usually wants to be able to offer the lowest prices.

And so on.

Anyway, after my students are finished telling what advantages they would most like to have I say to them: "O.K., I'll give you every single advantage you asked for. I, myself, only want one advantage and, if you will give it to me, I will whip the pants off of all of you when it comes to selling burgers!"

"What advantage do you want?" they ask.

"The only advantage I want," I reply, "is a *starving crowd*!"

Think about it.

What I am trying to teach you here is to constantly be on the lookout for groups of people (markets) who have demonstrated that they are starving (or at least hungry!) for some particular product or service.

How do you measure this hunger? Well, fortunately, if you are working with mailing lists, it is rather easy. Let's take an example: Suppose you want to sell a book on how to invest money and you have created a direct mail promotion designed to sell this book. Who do you mail your promotion to? Here are some possibilities:

Possibility #1—We could mail it to people whose names and addresses we get right out of a telephone book.

Comments: This is a terrible idea. There are too many non-prospects in this kind of group. The only thing in common that people in the phone book have is that they all have a phone. Some of the people won't have any money to invest. Some of them never purchase anything by mail. Some of them are too busy (or uninterested) to even read your letter. Some of them don't even know how to read! In short, there is too much waste circulation. This is like shooting with a shotgun instead of a rifle.

Onward.

Possibility #2—We could mail our promotion to people whose names and addresses we get from a phone book but only to those people who live in high-income areas.

Comments: This is a little better, but not nearly good enough. High-income areas are, incidentally, easy to identify because several companies have compiled statistics on every zip code in the United States, and they can tell you with great accuracy the average income per person in each zip code. They can also, by the way, tell you the average education level, average age, how much they spend on automobiles and a bunch of other stuff.

However, as I said, this still isn't nearly good enough. For one thing, not everybody who lives in a high-income area has a high income. Some of these people might be the maids or gardeners or some other type of servant. (Come to think of it, I'm not so sure that quite a few gardeners aren't wealthy.) Some of these people may have money but are not interested in investing. Some of them may always buy books from a bookstore and never by mail. Some of these people can't read English. (There are more and more rich foreigners in our country.) Some of them may have money to invest but are only interested in investing in areas in which they *already* have expertise.

Whatever. Once again we are shooting with a shotgun instead of a rifle. Once again, too much waste circulation.

Let's see if we can do a little better.

Possibility #3—We could mail our piece to a group of people who we are relatively sure have above-average incomes, like doctors, lawyers, architects, top executives, accountants, owners of expensive homes, and owners of Rolls-Royce automobiles.

Comments: Not bad. We are now getting into areas where we at least have a chance.

At least we are relatively sure that most of these people have a high enough income to maybe be interested in investing. Whether they are interested or not, we can't know, but at least, if they are, they probably have the *ability* to do some investing. This group of people is certainly more likely to respond to our pitch than the first two groups, but, as you shall see, we can do a lot better.

Possibility #4—We could mail our promotion to a list of upper-income people who are proven mail order buyers. Buyers of what, you ask? Actually, for the purposes of selling by mail, it is generally true that mail order buyers of *anything* are better than almost any group of non-mail order buyers. And, in this case, we have added the extra qualifications that they must be *wealthy* mail order buyers.

Comments: Now we are getting down to business. This is the first group I have described that gives us a reasonable shot at success. Not bad. Not bad at all. But now, let's stop fooling around and go for the hill!

Possibility #5—We could mail our promotion to a group of wealthy people who have ordered some other investment book by mail.

Comments: Bingo! Now we're cooking. What could be better? They are upper-income. They are mail order buyers. And they have purchased *by mail* a product similar to ours. What could be better? This is just about as hot a list as we can get!

Or is it? Actually, it is not. Let's keep trying.

Possibility #6—We could mail our promotion to a list of wealthy people who have purchased (by mail) a product similar to ours—*several times!*

Comments: Yeah! Now we're cooking! Just imagine. They're MO [mail order] buyers. They're wealthy! They've purchased (by mail) a product similar to ours. *And* they are *repeat* buyers of this type of product. How sweet it is! Can it get any sweeter? Yes, dear son, it can! Read on.

Possibility #7—We could mail our promotion to a list of wealthy people who have purchased (by mail) a product similar to ours—several times, *and who have paid big money for what they bought.*

Comments: Goody. These people are very close to the crème de la crème of lists we can mail to. But wait! Why do I say they are "very close" to the best? After all, what more could we ask for? Hold on! We're not done yet.

Not quite. Just keep reading.

Possibility #8—We could mail our promotion to a list of wealthy people who have purchased (by mail) a product similar to ours—and who have done so repeatedly—and who have paid big money for what they purchased—and who have *very recently* made such a purchase!

Comments: This is almost as good a list as we can get. It is certainly the best list we are likely to be able to rent.

But not quite. Just keep reading.

Possibility #9—We could mail our promotion to a list of people who have all the characteristics of possibility #8 *and which our friendly list broker tells us is working like crazy for other mailers with promotions similar to ours.*

Comments: For a variety of reasons, many lists that should work don't. Who knows why? It really doesn't matter why. What matters is that a list is or is not responsive. And the best way to know what lists are hot is to have a good relationship with a good honest broker. In fact, if you have a good relationship with a good broker, one of the things he will do (because it is to his financial advantage) is to keep an eye out for hot lists that are likely to work for your offers. And now, with this last list we have finally and truly identified the best list you can mail to.

Almost.

Yep. We can still do better!

Possibility #10—There is one group of people who will respond even better than all the other nine groups I have described. Can you guess what list this will be? Think about it a minute . . . [before looking at] the answer.

The best list of all is your own customer list!

Comments: All other things being equal, your own customers should respond far better than any other list you can get. Of course there is one caveat. They must be *satisfied* customers!

That's it for now.

I love you and good luck!

Dad

Friday, 7:09 A.M.
June 29, 1984

Dear Bond,

Well, here I am trying to get started again. Once more, I haven't the faintest idea of what I'm going to write about.

Let's see now. Oh yeah. When I left off last night one of the last things I mentioned was how the judicious use of parentheses (like this) can provide "eye relief" for your reader.

Alright. Now, let's talk a bit more about eye relief. Have you ever looked at a piece of writing and decided not to read it because it looked so forbidding? I'll bet you have. Many times.

Usually, this kind of writing will have long sentences, long paragraphs, narrow side margins, small type, and very little white space anywhere on the page.

Now, we certainly don't want people to *avoid* reading our copy for stupid reasons like this, do we? You say you agree? Good. In that case, I'll press on.

Now, listen up. When a person first looks at something you have written it should be something that looks inviting to read. Easy-to-read. When he looks at your page of copy he should be drawn to your copy like a convict is to a *Penthouse* magazine.

Your page of copy (be it letter or space ad) should be laid out in such a manner as to be an attractive "eye treat" for the reader.

This means wide margins, a certain amount of white space, double spacing between paragraphs, short words, short sentences, short paragraphs, and an attractive, inviting layout.

And now, my dear son, you are about to learn one of my most important secrets. What I am about to tell you is so important that you can get as much as 500 percent more readership. Yet, at the same time, this important consideration remains almost virtually unknown by almost every agency and advertising person I have ever encountered.

Listen up. Listen good, and never forget what you are about to learn. Here it is:

The Layout Of Your Advertisement Should Catch The Attention Of Your Reader . . . But . . . Not In A Way That Causes Him To Notice The Layout!

Actually, that's not as clear as it could be, is it? Perhaps I can do better. O.K., know this: In most publications, the editorial content gets five times as much readership as the advertising content.

Now, what does this mean on a practical basis? Simply this: It means that your ads should, as much as possible, have an "editorial look" about them.

(Better stop here and go call Blade and then go to "work." Maybe I'll get to rake the sand again today!)

Let's talk a bit more about the "look" of your ads and DM [direct mail] pieces. As I said, they should look (the ads) "editorial." However, they should not look like just any old editorial piece of writing. No. Your ads should look like an *exciting* piece of editorial material.

Here is a way to think about it: Imagine that you have written a book that you want to become a best seller. What's the best thing that could happen? Well, how about this? Suppose a guy who works as a reporter for the *L.A. Times* gets a copy of your book and reads it and falls in love with it.

Now, let us further imagine that this reporter likes your book so much that he writes a full-page article about your book and tells all his readers how wonderful this book is and why they should buy a copy. Wouldn't that be great? You bet!

And, just to sweeten things up even more, let us suppose that at the end of this "rave review" he tells his readers how to get a copy by mail. He tells them how much it costs, where to send the check or money order, and who the payment should be made out to!

Wow! How about that! A full-page rave review that makes the reader desire the book and then tells him where and how to get it!

Now my son, listen and listen closely. Whenever you write an ad it should look, insofar as possible, exactly like a rave review written by a reporter.

It should have the look of an exciting news flash.

Here's something else. You know, whenever I want to study ad layouts, I often study editorial layouts instead.

How do we apply all of this to direct mail? O.K., what would that reporter do if he wanted one of his friends in Hawaii to buy your book? The answer? Well, perhaps he would write his friend a letter and tell him the same things he told his newspaper readers.

And perhaps he would even include a snapshot of the book so his friend would know what to look for in case he wanted to go to a bookstore to get the book. This would be one hell of a sales pitch, wouldn't it? You bet it would, and that's how your DM letters should look.

Here is a true story. Once upon a time I wrote a letter to sell a product I dreamed up, which was a family name research report. This little report would give you a short history of your family name and it contained a black-and-white drawing of the earliest known coat-of-arms (family crest) ever to be associated with your name.

As you are aware, this became one of the most successful sales letters in history. In fact, this simple one-page 361-word letter generated more than seven million (actually 7,156,000) cash-with-order customers.

Not bad, eh? But listen to what happened next! Obviously, we wanted to sell these research report buyers other products, and the logical course of action was to send them a catalog showing a bunch of products they could get that would display (in full heraldic colors!) their family crest.

Sound good to you? It sounded *great* to me. So, what I did is I went off on a camping trip by myself and there, all alone in the woods, I created a $5\frac{1}{2} \times 8\frac{1}{2}$ four-color catalog which featured about 70 attractive items that could be ordered personalized with my customer's family crest.

It bombed.

It didn't even return our mailing costs! So, what next? Well, at that point, what I did is I took the three best-selling items in the catalog and I put together an $8\frac{1}{2} \times 11$ brochure that featured only three items.

It did only slightly better than break even.

What?

Groan. What to do, what to do?

Here's what I did then: I wrote a very personal sales letter and I enclosed a snapshot of the best-selling of the three items in the brochure. The opening of the letter went like this:

Dear Mr. Noble,

 I thought you might like to see what the Noble coat-of-arms looks like in full color, so I am sending you the enclosed snapshot.

Etc., blah, blah, blah, etc.

Forty million dollars!

 That's right kiddo. That letter brought in 40 mil while my other "more professional" attempts fell flat on their rears.

 What's the moral here? The moral is *you can do a better selling job when at first it does not appear you are attempting to do a sales job.*

 And, when I come back, the subject of my next teaching will be the importance of the fact that *you never get a second chance to make a first impression!*

I love you and good luck!

Dad

Thirsty Crowd Selection and Sneaky Second Glasses

David Garfinkel

David Garfinkel holds the unique distinction of being the first copywriting educator to put a multimedia training product on the Web, and has worked with businesses in 89 different industries. He has vowed to "eradicate copywriting illiteracy in the world" and is the founder of the World Copywriting Institute and executive publisher of Knowledge Exchange Press. David also is the author of several books, including Killer Copy Tactics *(Aesop Marketing Corporation, 1999), and has created advertising and marketing strategies for businesses that have brought in millions of dollars in new sales. His "single most impressive campaign" was a three-page sales letter for a business travel services company that added $5 million a year to the company's sales.*

To find out more about David's work, just type his name into Google. Warning: As of today, approximately 367,000 pages are indexed.

No doubt about it. The Great Formula is to marketing as the Great Wall of China is to walls!

The reason I like this formula so much is that it is the underlying basis of most successful businesses. Yet many businesses that are just limping along don't know the formula. It's good that this book is here to lay it out for them.

In my own business as an author, speaker, and teacher—and in my second business, as a consultant and copywriter—I've found several effective ways to discover what a crowd is thirsty for:

- Take careful note of what they're buying now.

- Listen to their *complaints* about what they're buying now. If they say, for example, "I like this mp3 player but I would also like to be able to download my e-mail into it," then—and this sounds pretty obvious, but you'd be surprised how many people miss this—*they're thirsty for an mp3 player that also downloads e-mail!*

- Find out what keeps them awake at night, what's on their mind the moment they wake up, and what's nagging at them in their thoughts all day long. It's usually expressed as a problem, which with a combination of common sense and marketing savvy you can translate into a picture of what they're thirsty for.

I created a product several years ago (curiously enough, at the suggestion of this book's author) called *Advertising Headlines That Make You Rich*. As a copywriter and a copywriting teacher, I knew that people wanting to write their own copy struggled endlessly to put together good headlines for their ads.

This product contained a series of templates with helpful guidelines and multiple industry-specific examples of each headline, tailored to a particular business in that industry. The product was a huge hit and a best seller.

Two years later, I realized that people were just as thirsty for the Second Glass of water—a set of templates for all the other parts of advertising copy besides headlines—as they were for the First Glass. So I created a second product, simply called *Copywriting Templates*.

I introduced this second product at an Internet marketing conference before I had even completed it. More than 40 people handed over checks and credit card numbers just to be among the first to have and use the completed product.

Since then, I've sold many, many more copies of this product.

What I just told you about is a fairly straightforward application of The Great Formula; let me give you a slightly more innovative example.

Recently I completed updating an out-of-copyright book by Dale Carnegie called *The Art of Public Speaking*. With my additions, the book will be rereleased as *The New Art of Public Speaking*, and I will be co-author of the book.

This is perfectly legal, because out-of-copyright works are in what is known as the public domain. Anyone is free to modify and publish that material however they want, as the copyright laws allow.

My publisher is Morgan-James. I mentioned to the founder of the company, David Hancock, that I thought a lot of other people would like to publish public domain works as well. I asked if I could go into business with him to help make those books available.

After some discussions, he decided to create a new division in his company, called Knowledge Exchange Press. He appointed me executive publisher.

You may ask: How is this selling people a Second Glass of water?

Well, it's subtle. But here's how it works.

In my book about public speaking, I tell readers that for a businessperson, the most valuable use of a speech is as a way to convey your marketing message with maximum credibility and impact.

And at the end of my (or should I say, Dale's and my) book, I now mention that an even *better* way to convey your marketing message with maximum credibility and impact is to publish your own book—like the one you are holding in your hands!

Then I will refer people to the publishing company that can make it happen for them.

So, the First Glass of water in this case is using a speech to bolster your marketing message; the Second Glass is using your own book.

To sum up, I'd like to point out that The Great Formula in its most basic application can mean the difference between profit and loss for a company, or, more typically, between just barely making a profit and making a huge one.

But when you apply creative business thinking to The Great Formula, you can create whole new businesses with a single idea. And that's why I like this formula so much.

How to Attract a $90,000 New Car

Dr. Joe Vitale

Dr. Joe Vitale, one of my earliest marketing teachers, is the author of Hypnotic Writing *(Aesop Marketing Corporation, 1998) and way too many other books and audio programs to list here. In my early business days I formulated my own business theory using my knowledge of psychology and military strategy metaphorically. When I finally began studying marketing in earnest, Dr. Vitale was my first teacher, and what a great choice of teachers! There are many charlatans masquerading as business experts, but Dr. Vitale came armed with the largest collection of marketing books ever assembled and a great track record for results. One of his direct mail pieces got a whopping 95 percent response rate.*

To find out about Dr. Vitale's current antics, you can visit his web site at www.mrfire.com.

I knew my latest book would do well because of the Irresistible Offer it made right in the title: *The Attractor Factor: 5 Easy Steps for Creating Wealth (or Anything Else) from the Inside Out* (John Wiley & Sons, 2005).

But I also knew that the first sale isn't where you'll find all the gold. The real treasure is in the follow-up, where you sell a Second Glass to a Thirsty Crowd.

What I did after my book hit #1 at Amazon.com and at Barnes&Noble.com (beating even the latest Harry Potter novel) was get my second cup ready for sale. I had a list of thousands of names, all buyers of *The Attractor Factor*. I knew they liked me, the book, and the ideas presented in it. This is my Thirsty Crowd. The next step was to create the second cup. Here's how I did it:

I quickly announced that I would hold a four-part teleseminar series called *Attract a New Car*. Obviously, everyone who liked the book would be interested in this new twist. And who wouldn't want a new car?

Now here's where I did something unique:

I allowed anyone to attend the teleseminar for free. I didn't charge a cent. This made people curious, it assured an audience, and it also guaranteed buyers. All the people who didn't make the calls would want to hear the audios sooner or later. So, of course, I recorded the calls. What I was doing was creating my next product.

I did the teleseminar and it was a blast. I had guests come on so I didn't have to do all the work. This made the process a breeze. I recorded it, had it transcribed, and turned it into a product.

Then I went to everyone on my list and said the audios were now available at www.AttractaNewCar.com. I sold the audios for $97.

How'd they do?

I made enough money to buy a brand-new BMW 645ci—a luxury sports car worth more than many people's homes, over $90,000.

Obviously, The Great Formula works.

To recap the sequence:

1. I began with The Irresistible Offer: my book itself.

2. I created a second product to sell the Second Glass: the teleseminar series.

3. I went to the list of hungry buyers and, yes, they bought.

I didn't stop there, however.

Knowing that everyone interested in self-improvement would be interested in my book and the follow-up audios, I paid for an endorsed e-mail to go to a self-improvement mailing list. The list consists of 250,000 subscribers. This is a Thirsty Crowd. I sent them an e-mail and they helped me earn tens of thousands of dollars from the sale of the audios.

What a beautiful formula this is!

A Personal E-mail from a Former BBDO Senior Vice President to Mark Joyner

Ben Mack

As a kid, Ben Mack was tutored by Buckminster Fuller, Dai Vernon, and Tarthang Tulku, and grew up to become a BBDO senior vice president. In 1998, Ben won an Effie award for the yo-yo craze that swept across American playgrounds, catapulting Yomega yo-yo sales from $6 million annually in 1997 to over $69 million in 1998 to over $123 million in 1999. He is the author of the foremost e-book on fire-eating, Fire Eating: A Manual of Instruction, *and is a pioneer in the burgeoning field of memetics, the study of thought contagion. He may, in fact, be the first person to introduce the concept of the meme to the marketing world. Ben's latest book,* Poker Without Cards *(Lulu Press, 2005), has been downloaded more than 300,000 times. His proudest business accomplishment was "The Bucky Challenge" in which Ben offered $23 to anybody who read his new novel and felt their time had been wasted, even if they downloaded the book for free. Over 100,000 copies of the e-book were downloaded during its promotion and only two people asked for the money!*

You can learn more about Ben by visiting his web site at http://pokerwithoutcards.com.

From: Ben Mack <Howard.Campbell@gmail.com>
To: "Mark Joyner" <xxx@markjoyner.name>
Date: Sun, 23 Oct 2005 23:09:11 -0420
Subject: Re: Thoughts on magic

Dear Mark,

Thank you for inviting me to contribute to your book. I am honored. But first, once again, you have created brilliance. In *The Irresistible Offer* you have simplified the essence of business: the offer and its acceptance. Wow! When I was a senior vice president at BBDO leading the strategy on Cingular, I wish I had thought of this simplicity. I would have been more effective.

I don't think *business* can be simplified further than you did in *The Irresistible Offer*: an offer and its acceptance. The simplicity of this insight will make many skeptical of its value. Those skeptics are wasting their time. Simplicity is a key to power because efficiency respects energy conservation. Waste leads to depletion. Mark, riddle me this: Why do so many people enjoy wasting their time with skeptical thoughts? Can you answer me that?

You asked me about how I find thirsty audiences. I rely heavily on Google. I have Google alerts set for my name, my book's title, and proprietary words I use in my novel, *Poker Without Cards*. When I get one of these alerts, I know I have an advocate speaking to a forum that is likely to be populated with folks thirsty for my wares. Many times I make an appearance and field questions while I encourage them to share with others the benefits of reading my book.

Googling "Google tips" will retrieve a page of various applications within Google. I regularly search for folks linking to my pages. With this I find discussions that have fallen through my alerts.

When I'm really hungry for thirsty minds, I go on www.amazon.com and www.bn.com and see what books people buying my book bought and then I use Google to find these thirsty minds and explain to them why my book has relevance to their interests. I have a very niched book, so I'm often scanning micro communities, either as myself or as an avatar. I never use my avatar identity unless a flame war breaks out. I've learned that all publicity is good. I was featured on CrapAuthors.com, and that coverage panning my book sold 50 books and another 800 copies were downloaded for free.

To drum up drama online I had two blogs running that were fighting with each other. Ben Mack was in a vicious fight with Howard Campbell, a fight that was launched by a Podcast with me obviously playing both characters. When there's drama, folks write about it. When they write about my drama, I join their conversations to extend the conversation. Over 300,000 have downloaded my book for free. I'm laying the groundwork for my next book, which *won't* be available for free. The title of my next book is simply: *23*. *Poker Without Cards* and *freeBookWorthReading.doc* explain exactly how *23* will be marketed.

I've been helping Steve Kaplan market his best-selling book *Bag the Elephant* (Bard Press, 2005). I have never met Mr. Kaplan, never e-mailed with him, never spoken with him on the phone. I imagine he has never heard my name. I don't really care about Kaplan. But his book marketer was somebody I wanted to learn from so I offered to help him for free so I could learn what he does. I offer to help folks I want to learn from. The help I give is with no expectation of immediate return other than what I learn in the process of helping. Magically, they wind up lending a hand when something appropriate comes along.

I've had a modicum of success with ezinearticles.com. I write an essay and it is pulled as content for various sites. Then, I know that site is interested in my kind of content and I contact them directly. Most of the time I never hear anything back. This is to be expected. I have a rule of two queries and then I don't contact them again for at least a month. I cover these details in a book entitled *freeBookWorthReading.doc*, a free book that is downloadable at my web site www .PokerWithoutCards.com. Mark, your readers need to know that while I go into great detail explaining marketing, branding, idea dissemination, and memetics, the beginning of *free-BookWorthReading.doc* is unintelligible to most readers. Readers who make their way through the homonym play and untraditional use of fonts will learn the exact tactics and strategies I have used. I know it is your rare reader who actually seeks to really work through your tactics, so I'm sure this won't matter.

Obviously, I'm not a best-selling author yet. But I have a list of endorsements worthy of bragging about and I explain exactly how I went about garnering these endorsements. Here are two that I'm proud of and I explain exactly how I got them. When was the last time you saw a book endorsed by Kurt Vonnegut Jr.? He just doesn't endorse books as a rule because he doesn't want to be barraged by requests. I explain exactly how I used Google Alerts and developed the relationship with Joe Petro III, a business partner of Kurt's. By tracking Kurt, I was able to repeatedly have an excuse to drop Joe a note. Google News and Google Alerts facilitated the excuse for contact that built the relationship that allowed me to get the quote you read below:

> "Ben Mack, Since you don't have the guts to be a homosexual, I'm glad that you are pissing off your parents by writing."
>
> **Kurt Vonnegut Jr.**
> *Cat's Cradle/Slaughter House 5*

Mark, I speculate that most of your readers will have no idea who this next guy is, but half my sales are probably due to the following quote. People consuming his words are my most thirsty audience. You studied with Robert Anton Wilson, so I know you respect his technology even if you don't subscribe to all of his politics or mine. In *freeBookWorthReading.doc* I explain how I got this quote from a legend of mental gymnastics:

> "*Poker Without Cards* is a consciousness thriller, combining natural philosophy with storytelling—the effect is like taking acid, only you never come down."
>
> **Robert Anton Wilson**
> *The Illuminatus! Trilogy/TSOG/Prometheus Rising*

Changing topics—In *The Irresistible Offer* you write, "The magic of marketing has to do with your own enthusiasm, belief, and confidence affecting your results. . . . I can say with reasonable certainty that what you expect will have a significant impact on your business." These words are evocative. I'd like to write about what these words mean to me. I'd like to write about *magic* and *marketing*.

I think magic deserves serious consideration, but I fear that this topic may be inflammatory.

On the one hand, magic can be seen as a tool of theatrics, a tool set that I have built for myself over the years. I started performing at The Magic Castle at the age of 14. At 19 the Academy of Magical Arts gave me an award, making me the youngest recipient in the history of the award. I get theatrical magic. But, I cannot fully articulate the magical frame of mind. I can say this: *When an audience feels safe, respected, and cared for, their minds loosen and their defenses drop*. Deception created purely for personal gain is a con, but immersive realities manifested for the benefit of the audience may feel magical.

Ad copy can be magical. Good copy respects the audience's values and sensibilities. Great copy communicates your love for your audience and their passions. You've helped teach me that if you don't love them, they won't love you back, and it's really expensive to go find new customers.

Magic is the act of facilitating an immersive experience, perhaps best encapsulated by the word *phantasmagorical.* Something is phantasmagorical when an audience transcends their skepticism and accepts a world where the laws of nature don't have such a firm grasp on reality. In advertising, copy can become phantasmagorical when it is stoking the passions of a diehard fan, helping them envision driving a golf ball 300 yards or bringing them into a moment of sports history that they can recollect with vivid details.

When copy is transformative, you have magic. The German philosopher Georg Wilhelm Friedrich Hegel said that an art object is a catalyst to an altered state of consciousness. Great ad copy takes us someplace else. Magical ad copy approaches the sublime.

On the other hand, *magic* can be a scary word. Last week, I was moderating focus groups among nurses and hospital employees of a children's hospital and the word *magic* came up, and a participant asked that we not use that word because it made her uncomfortable.

I suggest you be careful when you use the word *magic* or any of its synonyms. To many, the word *magic* evokes a threat of eternal damnation. To these people, a magician is a spiritual terrorist, striking out to infect the unsuspecting. There are more people who hold this to be true than I imagined as I grew up performing magic. Occasionally, some audience member would want to talk to me and get me to repent and save my soul. I can't quantify how many of these folks there are, what the incidence is, but the October 11, 2005, *USA Today* reported that 53 percent of Americans believe "God created human beings in their present form exactly as described in the Bible." If you figure half of these folks see the word *magic* as demonic, that's approximately one-fourth of all Americans. So the word *magic* should be used with discretion. Shakespeare reminds us: "The better half of valor is discretion."

So why discuss magic? There is real power in magic. And as *Lord of the Rings* taught us, the one who controls the magic controls the world. Besides, the danger of magic can be exploited for marketing, and so discussing magic can be profitable. Early twentieth-century magicians regularly employed images of demons and spirits on their promotional posters.

Besides, magic is real. Faith is powerful. A doctor in one of the focus groups mentioned earlier asked me if I knew what is the best predictor of success for patients about to have a critical surgery. I said no. He said the greatest predictor of success is the doctor's expectation of a good result. He said that mystifies doctors and that most won't discuss the studies that show that attitude has a physical manifestation on outcome, but he assured me these studies were real and had been adequately replicated to verify the findings.

I hold that prayer works. I also hold that the focus and intention are what work, not the specific phrases. I don't believe that some words are cosmic triggers. Hocus-pocus is just theatrical dressing.

Stigmatisms blight magical inquiry of the theatrical, let alone the spiritual. Inquiry into the unexplained is limited. Psi search publications are more often a joke than a contribution to science.

Early scholars of magic and perception were persecuted and killed. If I had used the word *executed* there, it would have depicted a government-sanctioned killing. If I had used the word *murder*, there would be an illicit connotation. Word choice affects how we process information. I see word choice as a form of magic since it can affect how we see things.

Words are powerful. Word choice is crucial. Scientology's flagship book *Dianetics* is littered with big words because L. Ron Hubbard wanted to intimidate his reader. Hubbard drew on techniques that perceptual scientist Aleister Crowley was developing. If you intimidate your readers, they are more likely to take you seriously. But the use of big words is off-putting to most. Hubbard wanted those taking his words seriously to learn these words. He explains that this then gives his followers a reason for better understanding how the world really works. I agree with a lot of his premise, but the whole alien thing throws me. But Mark, maybe I just don't see what he sees.

Being exclusionary is powerful. Those in the inner circle feel enchanted by their elite knowledge. Just look how profitable Pokemon was, a property built around big words that literally nobody knew until they defined their terms.

Magic theory is littered with big words like *prestidigitation*, a word intentionally made cryptic that means the act of quick fingers. Prestidigitation was coined by Reginald Scot in *The Discoverie of Witchcraft*, a sixteenth-century classic that attempted to disprove the existence of witches by detailing the charges against women who supposedly practiced the black arts. Scot wanted to present a scientific account of what these women were doing and so he used Latin, the language of science. *Presto* means quick, *digit* means finger, *ation* is the act thereof—prestidigitation, now known as sleight of hand.

The psychology of perception has not long been openly studied. Science that challenged the cosmography (worldview) of the Church was labeled as heretical, illegal, and often punishable by death. I reiterate: To this day, the idea of magic is offensive to many.

I respect the scientist Aleister Crowley I mentioned earlier. Crowley said, "We attribute to magick that which we don't understand." I fear I may be discomfiting you by my vocabulary. Marketing has a vocabulary. You learn the word *touchstone*, and presto, you communicate differently. I see that as magic. An opportunity has appeared to you. A technology has become visible. Vocabulary works like that. Vocabulary is magical.

I see value in cherishing moments that feel magical. I champion copywriters who can enchant their readers. I hope that my contribution to your book can dispel some of the misgivings around the word *magic*.

I love magic. I've been drawn to magicians my whole life.

But, I don't limit the term *magician* to a person doing tricks on a proscenium stage. Mark, you are a magician. I see you pulling money out of the air far more realistically than the stage trick entitled A Miser's Dream. I can perform A Miser's Dream. I can't make $50,000 in a couple of months despite having attended two of your seminars. You were gracious to include me, and these seminars have altered my life for the better. Next year, I might be able to replicate one of your tricks, using original patter and new accessories. Thank you for the empowerment. I can replicate some of what you do because you show me what you are doing. Most magicians won't do that as openly as you have chosen to do.

A magician is everybody who does something of value where I can't see what they are doing. They are using tools that I can't see. Mastery is a telltale sign of a magical mind. However, obsessive compulsions can also lead to mastery, while obsessive-compulsive thoughts rarely lead to tool invention. There is a loosening of associations that doesn't happen with obsessive-compulsive thinking. Your humor helps me focus while I relax into perceptions of reality where the insights garnered are new tools for my real world.

You are a science-based magician. You teach a science that facilitates magic. The heart of science is replication. I'm not speaking of viral replication or buzz marketing. I'm speaking about the scientific method, your ability to consistently replicate moneymaking experiments: magical acts of making money out of nothing, or so it appears to the uninitiated. But you have skills and you teach the skills and you appear again and do the trick one more time. You remind me of a young Al Goshman. who would repeatedly make a silver dollar appear under a saltshaker. He would make the silver dollar appear under a saltshaker 23 times in the course of a show. Goshman was a perceptionist, demonstrating that he could repeatedly misdirect his audience. But you aren't misdirecting folks. You are showing everybody how you do your tricks, how you pull money out of the air. Thank you.

Magic is not a thing or a physical act, but a state of mind that approaches the sublime but is more aptly referred to as phantasmagorical. Magic occurs at the intersection of a performer and an audience. There is intentionality to the perception. A stone that looks like an eagle is not magic, regardless of whether it is carved to represent the physical traits of an eagle. A sculpture may be a catalyst to an altered state of mind, but I am reticent to call a sculpture magical. Some panoramas feel almost magical to me, but real magic is dynamic and ephemeral. Magic is the process of engineering an experience where reality emerges as it cannot be, and yet the audience is compelled to set aside their disbelief and flow with the experience as long as it lasts.

Creating theatrical magic entails tweaking our visual prejudices. We drop a coin, and it falls. We know this to be true; we've seen the force of gravity pull objects to earth since before we had words to articulate the phenomenon. What most nonperceptual psychologists *don't* recognize is the extent that our mind projects our expectations, our visual prejudices, onto our sight. If a magician creates the physical gesture of dropping a coin from one hand to another, yet palms the coin so it doesn't actually fall into the second hand, most minds will see the coin fall. The term for this sight projection is *sight retention.* A normal mind will literally see the coin fall. This specific visual hallucination is called a projection; our mind projects its expectation of reality onto our sight. The magician makes note of the triggers that cause these visual breaks from reality and assembles a presentation that often includes a series of these triggers, often strung together through a narrative known as patter. The magician is an actor playing the role of a person with supernatural powers.

(The previous two paragraphs were swiped from a chapter I wrote for Dave Szulborsky's *This Is Not a Game* (Lulu Press, 2005), a book about using alternate reality games as Internet marketing vehicles, explaining in exacting detail how ilove bees.com helped make Halo II the biggest launch of any video game ever released. By the way, the concept of a swipe file has been greatly appreciated by me and many of my readers with whom I shared this valuable notion.)

Projection is a powerful force. Not only do we see what we expect to see, but often our expectations create our reality. The doctor mentioned earlier was explaining this dynamic, that a doctor's expectation of good results had a higher correlation to a patient's success than any other element tested. I would tell your readers what Grant Morrison recommended, "Fake it till you make it." My Bennington College buddy Bill Scully of VermontFineDining.com said that our college buddy Tom Dunn, a genius artist who is now being recognized, said, "Bill, we're finally doing stuff that is big enough to fit our egos." I've known Bill and Tom for 13 years. We each knew we were good. We also were regularly the only ones working at 3 A.M. Expectation drives determination, and hard work reinforces expectation. Grounded planning and stewardship of business plans helps. Scientifically testing your efforts and changing courses is worth the effort. Burning a colored candle is not likely to make money appear unless other preparations are in place, namely smart hard work.

If expectation of success is powerful, the willing suspension of disbelief is powerful. Theater and magic generate a willing suspension of disbelief, creating a magical frame of mind. Phantasmagoria is magic. A phantasmagoric effect generates a magical frame of mind.

Magic can be created from afar. A person who engineers a magical frame of mind, phantasmagoria, for an audience may or may not be a performer on a stage. If the person who engineers a magical experience is not the actor presenting the feats, it is the meme wrangler of the experience. Clock makers of the seventeenth century created automatons, mechanical men whose gears and riggings could be activated to perform the tricks of magicians. These clock makers were not magicians; they were the meme wranglers of their metal figurines that could perform magic, even in the absence of their creators.

Creating magic requires the recognition of stages within stages, seeing micro-stages within macro-stages. The macro-stage is the physical place where the audience encounters the magic. A magician may perform on a traditional proscenium stage, in a parlor, at a dinner table, or on a street corner—whatever location the magician interacts with the audience becomes the macro-stage. The micro-stages emerge as the audience shifts their attention. David Copperfield regularly performs coin tricks in front of audiences in excess of 2,000. How? He manages the micro-stages, the focus of his audience. By focusing his own attention, with all his body, on a silver dollar, he can command the attention of 2,000 sets of eyes, whose minds enjoy the representation of a miracle as he makes the coin vanish. Copperfield directs the focus of his audience. Site retention won't work unless the audience's mind is engaged. Not only must the mind see the cues that trigger the mental projections, but the mind must be so immersed in its focus that the mind accepts the magician's cues as real. The creation of these cues, the intentional use of projection triggers, is the keystone to invoking illusion.

Misdirection is the magician's ability to secretly do one thing by directing the audience's attention onto something else. Direction is the root of misdirection. Managing the micro-stages of an audience's focus is at the heart of misdirection; movement hides movement. How powerful is this technique? Harry Blackstone used to have an elephant walk on stage, upstage left, while he commanded attention downstage right. When Blackstone gestured upstage left, the audience was amazed to suddenly see an elephant. Rumor has it that this started as a bar bet where Harry wagered that he was so good at misdirection that he could walk an elephant onstage without any cover and the audience wouldn't even see it.

Meme wranglers are magicians, playwrights, screenwriters, and novelists, among other artists who create dynamic performances for the theater of the mind. The Internet has given birth to a new species of marketing theater; the weavers of magic who thread cyberspace into their tapestry are architects of a whole new set of possibilities and alternate realities.

Marketing has emerged as a legitimate face of perception study and the study of effectiveness, a socially acceptable way to understand magic theory. These techniques and discussions would have had us all murdered 200 years ago. The Puritans who founded America didn't suffer well the presence of alternative perceptions and realities.

Mark, enough about magic. How am I doing? Is this the type of material that might benefit your readers?

Touchstone—Here's what I'm working on.

Reading *Poker Without Cards* disengages your mind from *The Matrix* by explaining secrets of magic.

Poker Without Cards is written by Ben Mack, a child prodigy magician who grew up to be an advertising guru. *Poker Without Cards* debunks the popular ken, a consensus reality manufactured to cloud and enslave your mind.

By revealing principles of magic, Ben illuminates many of the smoke-and-mirror tactics of politics. By explaining the scientific techniques of mass persuasion, Ben presents the argument that our worldview is much more engineered than publicly documented.

I am Ben Mack. I also regularly post online as Howard Campbell.

I hold that you cannot see social engineering without a modicum or proficiency at persuasion and direct response marketing techniques. If you see the world as I do, you are actively contributing to a transformation to increase our likelihood of survival as a species. If you are active and want articulation as to how media work, read my book. Otherwise, don't waste your time. Keep up the good work.

If you don't like to read, I have worked with Chris Zubryd to make a video showing how masters of persuasion see the world. Google *The Pitch, Poker & the Public*, a 37-

minute video. The DVD has three hours of conversations with Jay Conrad Levinson, Mike Caro, Joel Bauer, and Howard Bloom.

If you think I am paranoid, then *Poker Without Cards* may change your cosmography. When you see the world differently, you will take action. I suggest you avoid operating heavy machinery for several hours after consuming my long-winded memes.

$28,000 Lying on the Table

Russell Brunson

Russell Brunson got his first real start as an entrepreneur when he purchased a product of mine two years ago. With his wife's permission, he put the $1,000 charge on his credit card saying he thought it would be a good investment. He now makes $50,000 a month at the fresh young age of 24. He has quickly positioned himself as one of the top experts in the field of Internet marketing, and deservedly so.

I think that I stumbled into the same trap that a lot of new entrepreneurs fall into when they first start. They learn how to generate leads and create sales but because of that immediate success they forget their existing clients and focus on finding new customers. Luckily for me, I asked a question that opened up a huge door for giving my existing clients a Second Glass.

I run a membership web site that has about 800 members who pay a monthly fee to be part of this community. I had focused for months on trying to add more members, when one day I decided to ask a question. I posted a message to our members asking if they would be interested in paying me $1,000 to show them how to better use their memberships.

Because I hadn't written a sales letter, created an order button, or even tried to sell this idea in any way, I really wasn't expecting much if any response. In fact, I posted the message not as something that I was going to do, but more as a question to see if they would want me to do it.

The first day after I posted that question, I received dozens of messages from people asking me where they could send the money because I hadn't included any way for them to pay. Within a week 28 people had sent the money for this coaching.

I was blown away at this response. There was almost $28,000 for the taking, and I just had to ask. Since then I have used this model to add back-end coaching programs with most of my products and services. The shift in my business has moved from having all my focus on acquiring new customers to spending more time working with my existing client databases. I am now making a lot more money and spending less time doing it.

The Gold Standard in Thirsty Crowds

Paul Galloway

Paul Galloway is one of the most influential software developers on the Internet and an Internet marketing technology consultant. He is the author of the Synergyx affiliate management system, which was hailed by e-marketing guru Dr. Ralph Wilson as the best of the breed. His short primer here on Standard Rate and Data Service (SRDS) will open you up to one of the most important marketing resources on the planet. He has also written two books, Selling on the Web *and* Online Business Resources *(both published by Made E-Z Products in 2001), and cites his proudest business accomplishment being the "integration of aMember, Synergyx, TAFPro, and Lyris into a comprehensive membership, subscription, and partner system strike"—any software programmers out there will know that this is no small feat!*

You can contact Paul at his web site at www.PaulGalloway.com.

Standard Rate and Data Service (SRDS; www.SRDS.com) publications are "must use" resources for the direct response marketer; they are *the* source for advertising media data, and all the professional advertising agencies subscribe to their service. A subscription to one of their publications can be several hundred dollars (depending on which publication you subscribe to), but they can also be found at most large public libraries. You may also be able to get an acquaintance in an advertising firm to give you their old copy when they get their new one (new issues come out several times a year). The SRDS publications of most interest are:

Consumer Magazines Advertising Source contains listings for more than 3,000 consumer magazines and card decks, including over 300 international magazines.

Business Publications Advertising Source has listings for more than 8,500 business publications, including over 1,200 international publications.

For each magazine or publication listed in the above two resources, you are given the following information:

Publisher's Editorial Profile	Classified Mail
Personnel	Order/Specialty Rates
Representatives/Branch Offices	Split-Run
Commission and Cash Discount	Special Issue Rates and Data
General Rate Policy	Geographic and/or
Black/White Rates	Demographic Editions
Color Rates	Contract and Copy Regulations
Covers	General Requirements
Inserts	Issue and Closing Dates
Bleed	Special Services
Special Position	Circulation

Direct Marketing List Source, the bible of mailing lists, is immense, containing over 19,000 listings in 212 categories—including co-ops and package insert programs! I highly recommend that you go to your library and just spend a few hours going through the pages of this fantastic resource. It's an excellent idea generator for your own marketing.

See how many lists there are related to your product/service. Perhaps you can adapt your product for national sales and distribution through the mail! You'll be surprised by the number of ideas you get just by going through this gem—plan on investing a minimum of two hours just looking through the various listings.

For each list, you are given the following information:

Personnel	Description
List Source	Commission, Credit Policy
Method of Addressing	Delivery Schedule
Restrictions	Fields of Specialization
Selections Available	Fees and Deposits
Mail Services	Test Arrangement
Letter Shop Services	Quantity and Rental Rates

The SRDS also has a publication titled *Newspapers Advertising Source*, which contains more than 3,200 listings of newspapers. Each listing includes the following information:

Newspaper buying reference material.

Market data by census region and by state, including population, households, effective buying income (EBI), and retail sales.

Standard advertising unit (SAU) definitions.

Newspaper representatives section, including newspaper groups and rep firms.

National newspaper listings.

Daily newspapers by state.

National newspaper classified rates and data.

Daily newspaper classified rates and data by state.

International newspapers.

Newspaper comics and newspaper-distributed magazines.

Weeklies and specialized newspapers.

College and university newspapers.

Black newspapers.

When you are ready to take SRDS to the next level, I highly recommend you read Gary Halbert's Boron Letters (available at his web site, listed earlier in this chapter) where he outlines some extremely useful methods for extracting money from these lists.

Former NASA Scientist Flies a Second Glass to the Moon

Harry "Hank" Johnson

Harry "Hank" Johnson is a former NASA scientist and the winner of the 1998 Body for Life Challenge, beating over 220,000 entrants to become crowned the Grand Champion. In 1999, Harry began selling the fitness program that he used to win the contest. He has since developed his own protein powder, Hank's Finest, and started selling Bastille Beauty Products in December 2004. Harry has helped hundreds of people get into the best shape of their lives and, because of his expertise in health and fitness, was invited to write a monthly column for Muscle Media *magazine in which he answers people's fitness and health-related questions. He is proud to know that he can "make a great living selling my information and products and, at the same time, help others improve their lives."*

Harry enjoys surfing, flying (pilot), exercising, and traveling. He lives with his wife of six years and son, Christian, who is now 17 months.

If you would like to learn more about Harry's work, visit his web site at www.healthfitnesschannel.com.

In 1998 I won the EAS Body for Life Challenge. I was 38 years old. After I won, many people contacted me asking for help on how they, too, could change their bodies. After the umpteenth time that someone asked me to help them get in shape, I realized I had found a Thirsty Crowd.

So, I wrote down everything I knew about getting into great shape. It took me two years to gather it together, and another seven years to refine it to where it is today.

I knew right away, even before I began selling it, that I needed to find something else to package it with. I couldn't sell customers my program again because once they learned how to get in shape I couldn't resell them that information. Sure, I could offer personal consulting (and this may be a very viable option for you), but I was still working for NASA and my schedule would not allow it.

So I started thinking. I thought back to when I was first getting in shape and asked myself, "When I was out of shape and overweight, what would have made it easier for me to get in shape?" So I thought about what I needed to do to help me get in shape. I knew that eating healthy, regularly spaced meals throughout the day was important. And I knew that I didn't have a lot of time to be cooking five or six meals per day. I knew that I wouldn't want to carry around this food wherever I went. And I knew that I would crave something sweet a couple of times a day. Then it hit me! I was already replacing some of my meals with a meal-replacement powder, but I didn't like its taste. I would create one that was great-tasting! Eureka!

So now I had the initial offer of my fitness program, and I followed it up with a Second Glass consisting of a protein powder that could be blended to make an inexpensive, great-tasting, convenient, and good-for-you meal replacement shake. And it took me only 8 years and 198 different tries.

Actually, I could have come up with this Second Glass a lot sooner, but I would have violated one of the underlying principles of *The Irresistible Offer*—to have a High ROI Offer. I could have slapped together a protein powder without regard to taste or composition of ingredients. But doing so would have been very shortsighted. And, by making sure I had a great product first, I fulfilled another underlying principle of *The Irresistible Offer*. Because I created a product that met or even exceeded the expectations of my customers (taste), I was able to make it a no-brainer for word-of-mouth advertising to happen almost automatically.

The important lesson for you to learn is that you need to spend the time to make a quality product if you want more than just a quick buck. When you do, you can create a truly impactful and truthful touchstone. Then, when your product truly does meet or exceed your customers' expectations, everything else will almost automatically fall into place. You'll have repeat business from existing customers, and they'll spread the good word about your product like evangelists. Create the great steak first, and then you can sizzle it to your heart's content.

Here's exactly how I did it:

First, I spent the time creating the great "steak." Then, since I knew that all I needed to do was get people to try my product and they'd be hooked, I offered to send them a free sample.

Think about how powerful this can be for exploding your sales (especially if your product lives up to your claims).

Your offer tells customers why your product is compelling (in my case my offer promoted my protein powder as the best-tasting protein powder in the world), and they don't have to risk even one penny in order to try it and see whether your claim is, in fact, true.

Remember that people are extremely skeptical about sales claims today. They're always asking themselves, "What's the catch?" So I made it as easy as possible for them to receive my sample so there couldn't possibly be any catch to it. I told them they could receive a free sample simply by filling out a form at my web site with their name and address, or call an 800 number recording and leave their name and address there. Notice that I subtly made them aware that there would be no human involvement in this transaction whatsoever. This overcame their skeptical barriers because they realized they wouldn't have to speak with anyone and potentially be subjected to a sales pitch.

Since I started offering this free sample, 67 percent of the people who visit my web site ask for a free sample. And 27 percent of those who receive a free sample then make a purchase. I offer those who do buy it a reduced price if they agree to receive it on a monthly basis. This has created an almost self-perpetuating increase in sales for me.

Concentrate on creating a good first impression with your product, and even if you don't have a way of selling them that product again (like my program), you can probably come up with another related product (like my protein powder), and your current customers will be much more likely to buy this Second Glass from you because you overdelivered on your First Glass to them.

How to Masterfully Persuade Your New Clients to Swig from the Second Glass— Even *Before* They've Sipped the First . . .

Or, Put a Better Way . . . How to Increase Your Sales by 200 Percent or More Instantly by Doing This One Simple Thing

Lee Benson

Lee Benson is among the cadre of young Internet entrepreneurs who, like Russell Brunson, have turned themselves into experts by proving their marketing skills on the electronic battlefield. By the time he was 21, Lee had sold more than $1,000,000 worth of product across various markets, and today his web sites receive over 2 million visitors a year. Since he first launched himself onto the Internet, Lee has created more than 25 successful web sites, tapped out more than 100,000 lines of computer code, written over 150 sales letters and more than 25,000 e-mail messages, recruited and motivated more than 17,000 individual affiliates, owned two companies, sold products to more than 50,000 clients, and spent more than 10,000 man-hours working solidly on the 'Net!

The technique Lee outlines here is similar to that used by Amazon .com on its order forms, but in a totally different context. From my experience I've found that adding the type of upsell Lee outlines for you here is more effective if used after the completion of the initial order, but this is a matter you'll need to test for yourself. Either way, you'll surely enjoy this story of a cool way to instantly snap a Second Glass offering into your Web initiatives. You can learn more about Lee at his web site at www.eliteinnercircle.com.

Throughout this guide the other Mad Scientists who have generously contributed their strategies, stories, and experiences with us have made one point blindingly clear:

The greatest money potential exists in quenching the thirst of your target market . . . *every time they're thirsty.*

That means giving your target what they want . . . constantly, and consistently . . . with a Second Glass, Third Glass, Fourth Glass, and so on.

What follows is one of my favorite techniques for enabling faster repeat selling. It's tried and tested, and the good news is that almost every business has the ability to implement it seamlessly into its sales platform. It's simple, and it could very well double your company's revenue.

HOW TO ASK FOR MORE MONEY—FROM THE FIRST SALE— AND GET YOUR CUSTOMER TO COUGH IT UP ENOUGH TIMES TO DOUBLE YOUR PROFITS

I call this strategy "Offering your customer a Second Glass before they've drunk from the First," and here's how it works.

Method for Using This Technique (Step-by-Step)

For this, I'll assume you already have a business selling a product or service of some kind. This is exactly what you do:

Step 1: Pull up your order forms (Web or paper), and identify what core benefits your product is offering the client. This should be easy—the sales literature that leads the prospect to this point gives you all the clues. Ask yourself: "Why is my client purchasing this?"

Think of two or three core benefits. Are customers pur-

119

chasing to help themselves? To help their business? To save time? To improve their golf swing? What other benefits would relate to this principal benefit that could co-factor into one *bigger* overall benefit?

If that doesn't fully make sense right now, you'll gain clarification in the coming examples.

Step 2: When you know the answer, pick another product that relates to the benefits of the first. If you sell golf clubs, you might think "educational golf video" (relating to the benefit of golfers wanting to increase their performance on the course). If you sell a business book, you might think "consulting" as a secondary avenue of supplementing the first benefit (which in this case may be aiding the reader's business).

If you sell vacations, you might think "travel insurance"—a benefit that relates to the overall vacation experience for the customer. Make sure it's something you already offer or can realistically begin to offer in the near future (and then take action to offer it).

Step 3: Take the price of that second product, and slash off the usual costs of acquiring a retail/full-price sale. Acquisition costs? They can go, since you've already acquired the customer. Advertising costs? Knock them off as well. Affiliate costs? No need for them here, either. Remove all price barriers (and perhaps a small profit margin) that usually stop you from pricing your stock lower. Aim for a price that's at least one-third lower than the original.

Why are you doing this?

You're going to offer this second product at the same time as the first (literally, on the order form). You won't need to spend money acquiring the sale, or advertising it. There's no sales commission to pay. All of the usual fees are buried in the price of your primary sale (the First Glass). Your secondary sale (the upsell or Second Glass) is devoid of these costs. Therefore, you can discount it.

The aim is to encourage the sale of the second product at the same time as the first. We'll see how in the following steps.

Step 4: Take your product, and modify your existing order form to include an offer for the new product as a small advertorial. Use an attention—getting headline inside that small insert that highlights the reduced price and the exclusive nature of the offer. Here are some examples I whipped up, for various products. . . .

For golfing equipment:
"You've bought the club, now learn to play! Buy *Secrets of the Swing* on DVD, and get an instant 65 percent discount off your order! Exclusively for first time buyers."

Business books:
"Hire the author to work with you in person—at 70 percent off his usual rate!"

Vacations:
"Now, save 30 percent off your dinner and theater tickets."

Software:
"Four new, never before seen features that will appear in version 2.0 upon its release in December. Here's how to get them, for 40 percent less than everyone else will pay."

Seminars:
"Bring your friend, partner, or spouse—for half price!"

Information products:
"Get the 'hidden extra chapter' that sold stand-alone for $997 to our closed-door group . . . for just $57 more."

Computing equipment:
"We'll unpack, set up, install, and configure your machine in under 60 minutes, guaranteed . . . anywhere in the country . . . for just $99 more!"

Web hosting:
"Is this site for business? If yes, process customer credit cards quickly and securely, FREE! (Just check the box.)"

These are just a few examples. They're not particularly imaginative, and you could do much better (although, for the five

121

minutes I spent conjuring these headlines, you may be surprised at the result). Tailor the headline, and the offer, to your product.

Step 5: Include a check/tick box in your ad, followed by the words "Tick the box to take advantage of this exclusive offer." or other effective action-inspiring wording. Include offer details but summarize the benefits—remember, this is a short ad. You're not writing a full-blown sales letter. You're hoping they'll check the box and put the form directly in the envelope to mail off . . . or click the submit button, if you're doing this on your web site.

Where do you insert the ad?

Somewhere the client *has* to look. I typically insert it right under the "payment options" area. When new customers have tapped in their card details on my order page, I like to make it easy for them to add this. I just have them click a check box to accept the upsell. It's super easy for them, and it has been shown—from my experience, at least—to boost profits significantly.

Step 6: That's it, you're done. Integrate the offer into your online ordering system (if you're Web-based) or have your printer make some new direct mail forms, and you're good to go. Or, as an additional test, you might even wish to try a *third* offer. That's something I've yet to try. Who knows? Test it and see.

Why does this technique work so well?

The answer, like every aspect of marketing, is in the psychology.

People love to save money. In addition, when an offer is "exclusive" or "one time only," they are getting something that the ordinary person wouldn't. You're selling to their ego.

The period between a customer consciously agreeing to make a purchase and completing/submitting an order form is a very special time. You catch them in a unique, excitable, frenzied state. They're already sold, so it takes very little to push them deeper into the sale. (Be careful, though—this can work in reverse. You can talk them *out* of a sale if you give them any last-minute reason to doubt. The prepurchase psychological consumer mind-set is a fragile one, to be handled with care.)

REAL RESULTS

The first time I tried the Second Glass technique of the *standard order form vs. order form upsell*, I discovered an astonishing 40 percent of people were ticking that box and taking the Second Glass offer. Since then, I've found 40 percent to be a conservative result. Often, the upsell option is taken by up 50 percent . . . 60 percent . . . even 70 percent of my clients!

What does this mean for you?

It means that almost *half* of the people who hit my order form purchased more in their first buying instance. And this happened without having to sell to them. The second offer piggybacked the benefits of the first. Every effort to sell them that First Glass had already prequalified them—mentally—to accept the Second Glass.

I made it simple for them. Just tick the box. Save the money. Reap the bigger benefit. And it worked—on average, almost half of customers chose to spend *more* money when given the option—without any extra promotion!

In other words, new customers were drinking from that Second Glass even *before* receiving the first. It was an instant pay raise.

My strategy works for all products and services, big and small, expensive and otherwise—from the lower-end items right up to the high-end, big-ticket items.

Here are a couple of real-life examples, to give you some inspiration.

Promotion #1: A $697 information course was coupled with a $397 upsell.

The web site saw 2,398 visitors and 44 sales, for a total conversion rate of 1.83 percent. Of those 44 new customers, 26 (59 percent) opted to take the $397 upsell by clicking the check box.

Gross revenue was up from $30,668 to $40,990 due to the upsell, and the average sale increased from $697 to approximately $931. The visitor value rose from $12.78 per click to $17.08.

This is as good as free money. And the best part? *The upsell was old, outdated stock*—still saleworthy, for sure, but in this case very difficult to position as a primary offer. What would have seen a response rate of maybe 1 to 2 percent in a "long copy" format saw a 59 percent uptake when coupled with another. *There was a 20 to 30 times better response with an ad that was 20 to 30 times shorter and less convincing in size.*

Here's the exact ad I used (only the unit totals have changed).

Save 66% off the Marketing Quickies™ license

Add another incredible product to your arsenal, for just ~~$1,191~~ $397 more!

We're only selling 5 more MQ licenses. Add this while you can!

☐ ◄ Check this box to add the Marketing Quickies™ license to your order, for just ~~$1,191~~ $397! This is the original license that made our holders over $150,000 in sales, and is still churning profits, *day after day*, for those who have this sales power.

Sell TWO products, and keep 100% profit.

Marketing Quickies™ is a two CD course that is still largely untapped and sells for as high as $197 per sale (and made over $150,000 in new sales!)

These CDs are packed with video tutorials that teach your clients fast, easy-to-implement, world-class techniques for marketing their sites online . . . *that we've used to pull $1m in sales!*

The license to this course sells for $1,191.00

But today, you can take it home for only $397—and have two amazing products to sell and cash in 100% profit on. Add this to your order; today!

Promotion #2: A $47 subscription received a $97 "gold" upgrade.

My friend wanted to try the same technique with his information business. The trouble was, he had only one product to sell—a subscription service he'd priced at $47 per month.

So, what did he do?

He took his basic product template and created a "gold" version of it. This was basically the same product with a few beneficial twists—extra tips and tricks not available to the standard subscriber, a little more support, and access to a gold members-only forum.

And he priced it at $97.

How did it do?

His order form routinely converts between 40 and 55 percent to the "gold" upgrade on a daily basis. One day last week, his site sold 86 subscriptions, and 38 took the gold. His profits for that day were up from $4,042 to $5,942—a $1,900 (47 percent) increase.

These are just a few examples. What could this approach do for your business? Try it and see.

This same concept can be applied to almost any type of order form—on the Web, and through direct mail. I've used it many times since, and every time, the same thing has happened . . . bundles of profits were scooped that would otherwise remain untapped.

FINAL THOUGHTS

I've been marketing for many years on the Internet. For the vast majority of this time, this tactic remained unknown to me—not through lack of creativity or scope of what could be done, but simply that *I never bothered to try it.* Inaction can truly be the costliest of all choices. Businesses that don't employ the mentality of upselling are missing out on perhaps the most profitable avenue their business has to offer.

How many more businesses are running on the fumes left by stale marketing ideas? At a conservative estimate, this technique would quite easily be worth seven figures to many of the businesses currently producing six . . . or six to those now making five . . . and in many cases, a business could be transformed from successful to wildly profitable with a little time spent crafting Second Glass order form upsell offers.

All from one dumb little check box, a headline, and a tiny ad on an order page.

It makes you think, doesn't it?

Secrets from the Blogosphere: How to Get a Lifetime of Loyal Readers, Subscribers, and Customers for Free!

Jason and Skye Mangrum

Jason and Skye Mangrum are a husband-and-wife team of market-ing virtuosity. They live and breathe market testing and have created some astounding results.

Jason is a joint venture specialist and contributing author to nu-merous best sellers, including The E-Code *(John Wiley & Sons, 2005), and the e-book* The Instant Traffic Formula. *He is also the co-creator of "The World's First Manifestation Software" (among others), and the world's first automated joint venture software, "The Instant Market-ing Miracle."*

Skye is a professional artist, Web designer, actor, musician, singer, songwriter, dancer, radio show host, and marketer extraordi-naire—it feels like there isn't anything she can't do. Her original ideas and concepts have played a major role in Jason's success and have made a positive impact on the lives of aspiring entrepreneurs around the world.

Jason and Skye currently live in Clarksville, Tennessee, with their two-year-old son, Aaron Amadeus Mangrum, and are expecting an addition to the family, Michael-Angelo Mangrum.

This article exemplifies the type of innovative work they are doing in the field every day. You can reach them at their web site at www.PassiveIncomeEmpire.com.

What universe are *you* from?

Where is your community? Okay. You've found The Irresistible Offer. Now where is your dehydrated market? Here are a couple of creative ways you can meet them in the middle of the consumer desert and offer them the first addictive glass of sparkling, refreshing water.

Welcome to the Blogosphere!

Meet them where they flourish, where they're already active and interacting. There are a couple of ways to meet up in the public gatherings of the Internet: blogs and forums.

I know you hear about these often, but they do work.

And here's how you can make use of them:

First, search Google, Yahoo!, Blogger.com, and tons of other blogging directories for blogs relating to your niche. Here's a way you can meet your target market head-on where they dwell. These are the folks obsessed with your niche—so much so they dedicate hours a day to writing, debating, and reviewing their biggest interest—your cash crop!

The quickest and easiest way to locate blogs within your target market is to use Blogger.com's new "Blog Search" feature at www.blogger.com/blogsearch.

Now that you've found them, take the time to comment— and if you like your niche this isn't going to be a chore. Answer questions. Give feedback. Include a little mention about yourself and your related product or site. Don't forget to mention where they can find you. If you provide genuine, helpful information, you've just gotten a foot in the fire. Be careful from this point on—you've just found the secret portal straight into the interactive community of your consumer base. Prepare yourself for tons of awesome feedback, product ideas (just pay attention; they'll tell you what their drink of choice is), and a myriad of ways you can fine-tune your product or service to be the best.

If you like to write, another way to get involved is to start your own blog. Become one of the community. Some of the largest companies in the world have started blogging their research, test results, product descriptions, and release dates. You can also obtain general information for any given niche from articles and news releases. But do everyone—including yourself—a favor, and encourage the interaction of your new community. Give your readers the ability to leave comments and subscribe to your RSS/XML feed. It's like having the ultimate opt-in, unblockable, very interested prospect list.

(*Quick side note:* You can find a list of the top 55 blog/RSS directories you can submit to for mega surges of quick and easy targeted traffic at www.masternewmedia.org/rss/top55.)

Now you know where to hit up the thirsty masses where they hide and multiply by the thousands every day. There are also a couple of new additions to the RSS world. Audio blogs—often referred to as Podcasts—give listeners the ability to subscribe to your audio feeds and listen to your lovely voice on their computers or download it onto their portable MP3 devices.

And the latest development—which has not yet been used for any real marketing purpose—is video blogging. Mostly in this format you find individuals recording and posting their personal journals and short films. For someone with strong vision and lots of passion and creativity, here's your opportunity to burst this subscription format wide open.

You've got your foot out and prepared for the blaze. Be sure to submit your blog (if you make one) to the various blog directories, giving yourself overnight surges of free targeted traffic. Don't forget to include shameless promotions in your posting.

It's also a good idea to have a separate main site that links to your blog, and vice versa. Have a capture or gateway page to your main site. This is not a pop-up, but more of a special offer and a name and e-mail submission area. Visitors click the "Sign me up" button and are directed to your home page from there. So this is the setup process, and there are two ways it can go down:

1. Prospects are online reading your blog via your RSS feed, or your comments you leave on related blogs, and want to know more, so they check out your main site and land on your squeeze page. They enter their name and e-mail and are now in your autoresponder for follow-ups. Then they are redirected seamlessly to your main page, sales letter, or other direct offer.

2. Traffic is directed to your web site through other means (paid sources, search engine optimization, articles, and referrals). They first hit your squeeze page, where they enter their name and e-mail—adding them to your autoresponder. From there they are directed to your main site with your sales letter and main information. From there they can link to your blog, where they can get to know you and read all the articles you've written. Prospects can contact you and add ideas, and they can subscribe to your RSS feed (aka the ultimate opt-in list).

What's the point to all this?

Multiple points of constant bombarding contact equal instant top-of-mind awareness. You're everywhere. And guess what? Poof—you're an expert!

- Prospects who sign up to your squeeze page (proven to be wildly successful when list building) will begin receiving e-mails from you right away.

- Your web site is now linked to constantly updating content via your blog, and you're encouraging repeat traffic.

- Prospects who visit your blog and like your content will subscribe to your feed, and every time you post they will be notified to come check it out, or your entire post will show up in their aggregator or feed reader.

We have recently started to test and track one of our main sites with this awesome formula. It has the capture page system with the main site linking to a blog that is updated with both automated articles and hand-submitted content, as well as affiliate test results and reviews (see www.JasonMangrum.com).

Of course you need to be keeping track of where all your traffic is coming from and what their actions are. We use several services to submit, track, and promote the site and blog, and guess what? You can find all the sources we use on our blog at http://tested-affiliate-marketing.blogspot.com.

As for the Second Glass, what you've created here is a *lifetime* of contact with your target audience. A blog in itself creates a direct personal connection with your prospects. And it's easy to keep it updated. All you have to do is keep your contact list up to date with every new product you create using your autoresponder and your updated blog. This can also be a very easy way to promote any related products of which you are an affiliate.

There's your Second Glass sold, as well as the Third Glass (and as many others as you choose to promote), to your constantly growing list of readers!

In the past, squeeze pages and other methods of rapid list building have created the perfect conditions for the Second Glass offer.

The gold really is in the list. Past customers and prospects alike are privy to the back-end offer through e-mail follow-ups.

Simple, direct, and constantly growing—now there's an unblockable follow-up system via your blog. (Plus, you'll never receive a spam complaint with your blog's RSS feed, and you'll never have a problem with deliverability, either!)

We are the guinea pigs in these and other methods of rapidly changing multimedia promotional formats. You can see all of our adventures, tests, and pure unadulterated results at http://tested-affiliate-marketing.blogspot.com.

How Two Magic Words Can Almost Guarantee Your Customers Will Be Practically Begging You for a Second Glass

Yanik Silver

Yanik Silver's friends laughed when he told them he was going to put up a web site back in February 2000, and they had every right to be skeptical—Yanik had no web site design skills, scant computer knowledge, and zero HTML or coding ability. But that didn't stop him from going ahead with his simple two-page web site. In just a few short years, Yanik has sold millions of dollars' worth of online product ranging in price from $17 to $14,500, and all with only one employee: his wife Missy. He has also built up a team of 36,773 affiliates during a time when the pioneers of online marketers had already established their networks. It is little wonder that Yanik is now recognized as one of the leading experts in the field. When he's not busy cranking out new projects, Yanik enjoys traveling and playing beach volleyball, ice hockey, and just about any kind of extreme sport he can find.

The following article demonstrates why Yanik is currently marketing legend Dan Kennedy's resident Internet marketing expert. You can also contact Yanik at his web site at www.surefiremarketing.com.

Back in 2001 I almost stumbled onto this secret. . . .

You see, that was when I first released a viral electronic book (e-book) that was meant to be passed around on the Web. That part worked great. In fact, I just went to Google today (October 16, 2005) and typed in the name of the e-book *Million Dollar E-mails* in quotes and it still came up with 72,200 references more than four years later. Now that's 72,200 web sites that are selling, giving away, or mentioning my e-book—so I can only imagine how many countless copies are circulating on the Web.

But this isn't the point. The point is the two magic words, right?

I can almost hear you screaming, *"C'mon, Yanik—give me those two words already, bub!"*

I promise I will, but not quite yet.

Let's fast-forward a few years to 2003 and I've pretty much forgotten about my little e-book adventure and the fact it included the "two magic words" on the cover (oops, there's a hint). You see, I was considering the idea of coming clean about a hidden way to literally steal an almost endless source of content (on practically any subject you could imagine). I teach ordinary people how to successfully sell materials like e-books, manuals, audio programs, and DVDs online—something called "information products marketing." But unless you've been exposed to this specialized concept of selling information you wouldn't think it was even possible since most people believe everything is free online. It's shocking to most people when I reveal my students selling everything from potty training info to guitar lessons to investing information online and making six-figure incomes with their little ventures.

However, one of the big problems and concerns I heard all the time from struggling students was something like: "I don't have any ideas for what to sell" or "I don't have time to create information to sell." Bingo! Anytime your customers or prospects gripe about something, that should be when your ears perk up because there's lots of money to made giving them your Irresistible Offer.

That's when I decided to go ahead and hold a two-hour tele-conference call to spill the beans about how I'd been able to tap into this mountain of public domain information for years and years. Plus, I asked a legal expert and two other guests who have had success with public domain material to be part of this call.

After setting up the details, I made a quick announcement to my subscribers and the response was crazy. I thought I'd need maybe 150 to 200 phone lines, but I sold more than 850 seats to this teleconference call at $49 per spot (or $97 if they wanted an audio CD sent to them). For about two hours of work I made a tidy $47,926, but more importantly, I knew this had hit a major hot button.

That's why after the call I simply asked the 800-plus attendees one question: "What is the one lingering question you still have about finding, using, and profiting from public domain?"

Here's the e-mail I sent:

What's your biggest question on public domain?

Hi [firstname],

After the "Public Domain Riches" teleclass I received a ton of great feedback like this:

"My head kept buzzing, and after the call I was searching some of the web sites you mentioned and I've now got an idea to run with. In fact the call ended at 10:30 p.m. my time and I went to bed around 5:30 in the morning! Like everyone else, I always knew about public domain works but never in any detail. Thanks to your call I can say that finding the work I'm interested in took only about 20 minutes, and a simple e-mail confirmed that the work is in the public domain and I can use it as I want! . . . I came away with at least 10 times the value before even doing anything."
—Moragh Pitt, Orpington, Kent, UK

"Prior to the 'Public Domain Riches' call, I had many questions concerning copyrights and public domain works. [You] made sense of it all for me and now only one question remains. Whatever will I do with all the money I'll be making?! Honestly, while on the call, which lasted for two and one-half hours, I came up with eight different ideas for information products. If only it had been a four-hour call!"
—Joi Sigers, Charleston, IN

But even with all the wonderful comments I still want to do even more. That's why I'm putting on an absolutely FREE teleconference call to answer the most pressing questions you still have on finding, using, and profiting from public domain.

So go here and ask away:

[URL]

We'll be e-mailing everyone with the phone call date and time to listen in as soon as it is scheduled.

Also, just to let you know if you ordered the Gold upgrade your CDs and written transcript have shipped today, so be on the lookout for them. (And if you have not received the digital download information for some reason, let us know.)

All the best,

Yanik Silver
SurefireMarketing.com

P.S. That link again to ask your question is:

[URL]

Okay, this was nothing fancy, but the responses and answers I got gave me the idea for a Second Glass. They told me there needed to be a much more comprehensive and advanced program that took people step-by-step through the process—from finding and selecting public domain works to exactly how to profit from them. I decided to hold a private e-class for 15 people in which I delivered lessons and homework assignments via e-mail for eight weeks to attendees. (This e-class sold out five separate times until I stopped offering it as a live course and turned it into a home-study course.)

Now on top of the requests for more advanced help, the responses we got from the survey also centered around the questions "How can I be sure a work is really copyright-free?" and "How can I find a good market or niche to sell information to?"

After reading those questions, I decided the next thing I'd offer in the "Public Domain Riches" family would be something I named "Public Domain Goldmine™." This product was a "fish." You've certainly heard the expression about "Give a man a fish and you feed him for a day. But teach him to fish and you feed him for life." Well, people today are busier than ever and they don't want to learn how to fish. They'd rather have their fish grilled and served them on their plate ready to eat with a little mango chutney on the side.

"Public Domain Goldmine™" consists of 35 public domain works in 35 different niches handed to the customer; each work has had its copyright cleared by an attorney and it has actually been scanned in (so people can edit and manipulate the text). Plus it includes spreadsheets of search engine keyword research, market analysis, competitors, back-end products to sell, possible joint venture partners, and more. Like I said—this really is the "fish" with everything done for the customer.

Now I had a really big feeling this would take off, so I wanted all the original "Public Domain Riches" customers to get a fair shake at it. Here's the e-mail we sent out to them letting them know something was coming down the pike:

Advance notice for Public Domain Riches customers

Hi [firstname],

Yanik Silver here from PublicDomainRiches.com.

I wanted to give you advance notice to look out for an e-mail coming tomorrow (Wednesday, May 19, 2004) at exactly 12:00 Noon, EST (New York time) with the subject line of "Public Domain Goldmine is here."

Keep your eyes peeled because that next e-mail is going to give you all the details on the ultimate "done-it-for-you" niche information marketing package. This grueling project took months to create so you can turn around and immediately profit from it. In fact, my partner and I shelled out well over $6,890 in cash and poured over 150 man-hours into putting all this together for you.

Now after all this hard work there's no way I'm letting the whole world get their hands on this. That's why only 250 packages will be available.

But instead of just springing this on you guys, I figured the only fair thing to do is give everyone advance warning, especially because we have customers in all different time zones and countries. (My partner is doing the same with his best customers.)

With that said, tomorrow when the doors open, I predict even more chaos and mayhem than Janet Jackson's "wardrobe malfunction" during the Super Bowl. So if you want to grab one of the 250 packages, watch for that e-mail announcement.

I promise you won't be disappointed when you see what I've got up my sleeve—but I'm keeping quiet about all the juicy details until tomorrow.

All the best,

Yanik Silver

Let me step back for a moment and talk about something that might not be apparent here. It's the same secret any big blockbuster film or releases uses—and that's anticipation. Maybe you remember the excitement building for *Star Wars* or *Harry Potter*? It's the same thing here but on a smaller scale. Yes, this was short notice but it still served the purpose to give them a heads-up that something big was coming.

The next day when we announced the product (as promised) and let people order, our sales went through the roof! We brought in $71,624 in less than 48 hours and we sold out all 250 packages available in nine days flat!

And we went on to sell out every other "Public Domain Goldmine™" package that's been released since this first one. In fact, the longest time one has been on the market so far has been 13 days.

How? A big part is using those two magic words I've been teasing you with.

Okay, ready to hear them? Drumroll please. . . .

They are: **"Volume I."**

That's it. I know it seems almost too simple, but if people

like your Volume I, guess what they'll want? Of course, Volume II, III, IV, and so on.

Really, this has tons of applications if you give it some thought. Here's a quick example from Hollywood. Think about Quentin Tarantino's recent film *Kill Bill*. Quentin shrewdly set himself up a built-in audience for the sequel because he named the first film *Kill Bill: Volume I*. Hey, I went to go see *Kill Bill: Volume I* and then afterwards I had to see the complete story by going back to the theater and plunking down my money again for *Kill Bill: Volume II*.

By automatically setting up sequels you can get your customers practically begging you for a Second Glass (or a Third, Fourth, Fifth, etc.). And that's exactly how you get rich and serve your customers at the same time.

Find Their Thirst Through Criteria Elicitation

Kenrick Cleveland

Kenrick Cleveland has been the go-to guy and secret weapon for persuasion training for more than 22 years. He has instructed more than 10,445 "in the trenches" persuaders on how to gain clients' trust within three seconds, how to eliminate objections (before they have a chance to materialize), and how to close a sale so elegantly that customers feel confident in their decision to buy. Kenrick's clients have reported up to 407 percent increases in sales, and up to 352 percent increases in income, just from employing his techniques. Most notably, Kenrick used his strategies for influence and persuasion to help train the trainers (those responsible for staff education) at Home Fed Savings and Loan (now known as Home Fed Bank). His methods were applied to every level of the corporate hierarchy—from vice presidents to the tellers in the banks—and have been credited with increasing Home Fed Bank's net deposits by $1 billion!

You can reach Kenrick at his web site at www.maxpersuasion.com.

One of the power techniques that I have used for one-to-one selling (and that I have trained thousands of other people in—to rave reviews and spectacular increases in income!) is the use of criteria elicitation. Criteria elicitation is basically getting the person's values about the specific product or service that you are selling, and then ethically matching those values by describing your product or service in the exact words the client just gave you.

I really exploded my own business when I applied these techniques to selling into a crowd or market.

Criteria elicitation—on the surface—is a very simple process. Applied to a crowd to find the thirsty, dry, and parched prospects, it involves asking:

"Why are you here?"

They will answer and provide the need that they are looking to fill.

To give you a reference point, let me also describe how it works in belly-to-belly selling. For instance, in person, if we were meeting to explore your buying, say, real estate (or any other thing or service) from me, I would start out by asking you:

"Why are you here today?"

You will answer with a statement answering this question, like:

"We're just finding that our house is too small. I have my business at home now and with the kids still at home and running around all the time, it just makes it really hard to concentrate like I have to, to do the best job I can."

APPLIED TO A MARKET OR CROWD

You would first create a database of people who have responded to an online ad and/or a newspaper or magazine ad. You may already have this list of people who have bought from you or have inquired about doing business with you.

You would then make a simple telephone call to a person who is in your target crowd with the question "Why are you looking for financial advice (or real estate or a widget) today?"

And they will answer. It is really important to record exactly what they say, because this information they give you is profit gold! Or they might answer, "Well, we are just looking at the real estate companies around here and wanted to check out your service."

And you would ask again, "Okay, I understand, but why now? Why are you checking into real estate companies now?"

And they will answer (again record exactly what they say), "We are expecting a new child and need to get a bigger house" or "We just retired and are looking to downsize our home" or whatever.

Then you would answer, "Yeah, that's a good reason to move, isn't it? I can understand why you would want to check into real estate right now. But just so I really understand your needs so I can make sure we are on the same page, what's important about downsizing your home?"

It is critical that you use the words that they provide to you and feed them back by asking "What's important about X?" This is what digs out their first-level values—the criteria that are of utmost importance to them.

And they will answer, "Well, we don't need all that space and we also want to downsize so we can take some of the equity out and still have a nice smaller place and a more secure retirement."

And then you would answer, "Wow, that sounds good, doesn't it? I can really understand that you folks want to still have a nice smaller place and have a secure retirement. Awesome. That looks really good. And tell me, just so I really understand where you're coming from, what's important about a nice smaller place and a more secure retirement?"

Again you are repeating back to them exactly what they have said. This is the second level of criteria. (You are writing this all down as they give it to you.)

And they will answer again, "We want to travel and see all the places that we were never able to before."

And you would answer, "Yes, yes. That feels really right, doesn't it? You want to travel and see all the places you were never able to. Now, I'm just curious, and this will really help me to get you the perfect place and help you reach these goals. Ultimately, what's important to you about travel and seeing all the places you were never able to?"

And they will answer, "Well, it's just what we've always dreamed of doing. We've always wanted the freedom to just go to all the places like Tahiti and Australia."

"Awesome. That's an awesome dream, isn't it? Wow, thank you so much for sharing that with me! That helps me so much to be able to get you what you want."

And now you feed their values back to them while you describe what you can do for them so that all they see, hear, and feel is that you are giving them exactly what they want—in this case downsizing their home to have three benefits:

1. A nice smaller place and a more secure retirement.

2. The ability to travel and see all the places they were never able to.

3. The freedom to just go to places like Tahiti and Australia.

(Describing this process is always a bit limiting. In reality it's an amazing thing to get this information from prospects and then watch their faces absolutely beam as you feed it back to them tied into what you are selling. It really is an amazing experience.)

There's a couple of points here that I want to make before we go further. First, it is critical that you allow the prospects to say (or write) what is important to them. If *they* don't express it, it's not anywhere near as powerful! Do not guess.

Second, it is just as critical that you repeat what they've said *exactly*—no interpretations or active listening. None! Get creative here and you'll be disappointed. Repeat their words back accurately and you create magic.

So to use this in your presentation you would frame your presentation around the values they have given you:

"Now, one of the things that I have had some experience in is helping people downsize to a nice smaller place. And that sounds like something that would be critical for you so you could travel and see all the places you were never able to. And I bet you'd love to feel the freedom a new, nice smaller place would bring to go to places like Tahiti and Australia. How does that sound?"

Repeat this criteria elicitation for 20 to 25 of your customers and you have a database diamond mine of the deep values of your market. More important, you have the words to use that will strike deep into their thirst and compel them to do business with you!

Other ideal places to gather this critical information would be at trade shows, at malls, with an online blog, and the like.

Look for the words and values that are repeated across the people you have interviewed. Those are the values and words to concentrate on in your marketing letters and pitches. You also want to include as many of their values and words as you can to expand the net as wide as possible.

Hard-Coding the Minds of Your Prospects for the Second Glass

Joshua Shafran

Joshua Shafran is known by many as "The 30 Million Dollar Man" because that's how much he has made for his clients over the past four years as a direct marketing consultant. Early on, Joshua recognized the importance of testing and did thousands of side-by-side marketing tests (A/B split testing) to discover what worked and what didn't. As a result of this work, he was able to mastermind and pioneer a variety of innovative new online marketing methods. Today, many of these methods are recognized as standard operating procedure. More recently Joshua created a business building system known as Net Profits on Demand (NPOD) that has fans raving the world over and has earned himself the additional moniker "Mr.Npod." In less than two years, Joshua successfully trained up to 2,000 people with his unique NPOD system (and that's no small feat considering that he started from zero and the NPOD training system was priced at $500!).

You can learn more about Joshua at this web site: www.The2 CommaClub.com.

Let's talk about exactly *how* you can create and actually *install* a buying mind-set into your first-time customers (just as you would install a software program on your computer) so the "Sell them a Second Glass" part of Mark's Great Formula is a hard-coded part of your business model and processes.

(*Side note:* These techniques work just as well in helping you get the first-time sale (selling the first glass) as they do in setting up the Second Glass sales. The power of what you're about to discover in this section will allow you to create a business asset that spins off tons of profits *every month* in Second, Third, Fourth, Fifth (and on and on), Glass sales. This is the secret of how very small customer/inquiry lists can produce amazing profits month after month, like clockwork.)

Very few entrepreneurs and businesses truly understand both the art and the science of this process. Some (not many) use it but not intentionally, while the majority of businesses (even successful ones) don't use it at all because they don't understand its power.

See, it's all about the relationship you create. Actually, more accurately it's all about the *perceived* relationship that your customers (and potential customers) *feel* they have with you. It's about communicating in a way and a unique style all your own that *bonds* and endears you with your database on a real human level. It's about creating a feeling with every single one of your customers (and would-be customers) such that they feel they personally know you.

Almost like you are a close personal friend of theirs (even though they've never met you and probably never will), you want them to feel that they are a part of your inner world. When you get this right, they start to feel like they've known you (or wish they had known you) forever. You become that long-lost friend that they can pick back up with as soon as you guys find each other again.

This *bond* you create becomes your most powerful business asset because you can leverage it into amazing wealth, prosperity, and freedom. It's your business's secret currency.

See, out of this bond, you create a deep connection with your customers, clients, and prospects that is almost immediately and automatically converted to trust. Once people trust you, they will buy from you . . . and not just once. No. They will buy your products, services, ideas, and endorsements again and again and again so long as you don't do anything to

145

break that bond. And, this, of course, is what Mark's "Sell them a Second Glass" part of the formula is all about.

Here's an often overlooked fact: We tend to trust people we think are just like us, who have the same ideas, values, and opinions toward things. Here again, we're talking about building the bond.

See, this is how really great marketers, businesses, and entrepreneurs build empires. There's a direct marketing concept called lifetime value (LTV) of the customer. Simply put, this is the total amount that a customer will spend with you over the life of his/her business relationship with you. Say your average customer buys from you three times a year, spends an average of $200 each time, and will stay with you an average of five years. In this case the LTV of your average customer is $3,000 (every new customer is now worth $3,000 to you).

Get how it works?

Okay, now stick with me here because here's where it gets *good*, and it also happens to be where most people *stop* in their understanding of these principles. What if you were able to bump the number of annual purchases up a bit (sell them just one more glass of water) and at the same time you were able to increase the size of each transaction (make it a super-sized glass of water) *without spending any additional time, money, or effort?*

Let's go back to our example three paragraphs back. Say you are able to bump the average yearly purchase from three to four and increase the size of that purchase from $200 to $250. Now over the same five-year period that customer is going to be worth $5,000, instead of only $3,000! *That's almost double from the same customer!*

See, there's a natural portion of every database (generally it's a fairly small percentage) who will buy from the company/person again and again. In direct marketing terms we call these people "hyperresponsives"—these are the valuable customers who want everything you've got. Generally, if you don't do anything at all, 4 to 5 percent of your database will fall into the hyperresponsive category automatically. But there's a way you can substantially increase that percentage above where it naturally falls. I've been able to increase it to levels around 20 to 30 percent, and I know of marketers who have gotten their percentage of hyperresponsives as high as 50 percent.

How?

Through the bonded relationship you create with your database.

Believe it or not, it doesn't take hundreds of thousands of new customers to make yourself a fortune when you know how to properly build this bonded relationship that creates hyperresponsive buyers.

Now let's move right into all the insider secrets of *how* you tap this bonding power yourself.

ROMANCE 'EM, SEDUCE 'EM, TEASE AND TANTALIZE 'EM . . . BUT DO *NOT* PROPOSE *BEFORE* YOU GET THE FIRST DATE

Have you ever been romanced? Have you ever been the one doing the romancing? The process of selling somebody something or bonding with them is a romance of sorts. It involves building a relationship so that there's trust present, and then the prospect is *open* to stop what they're doing long enough to listen to your Irresistible Offer with an open mind (instead of automatically tuning you out as they would if the same offer didn't come from a trusted friend). When you have their undivided open-minded attention they are much more likely to want to purchase, or to believe, or to buy into whatever your idea may be. This is the job of your sales letters, free reports, television commercials, infomercials, radio interviews, newspaper ads, products themselves, web sites, free training courses, e-zines, or any other systemized communication medium/method you utilize.

Maybe you're selling a particular idea, maybe you're selling why they want to be a part of your database, or maybe you're making a direct offer for a product or a service . . . whatever it is, you're selling. That's what really good marketing is: salesmanship multiplied and systemized! See, your marketing becomes an *army* of the best salespeople in the world and does the relationship building, bonding, and selling *for* you.

Now, contrary to mainstream thinking, cutesy slogans, stuffed animals, sock puppets, Chihuahua dogs, or any of the other funny things do *not* constitute systemized salesmanship! All those things are the equivalent of the adolescent boy going right up to the homecoming queen that he's never met before and saying "Let's go to my car and do it"—chances are he ain't gonna get the result he was hoping for.

Here's another less crude example. Say you're going out on a first date with someone. You wouldn't immediately ask her to marry you as you pick her up and walk her to your car, would you? No one seems to be attracted to desperation. I suppose that occasionally this type of approach will work, but it certainly isn't a surefire way, is it?

See, it's about romance. You can't rush it. You've got to let it build, let them come to you . . . tease 'em . . . play hard to get. Build a relationship. Create that bond . . . trust. You've got to give them a good reason to do business with you. And that's a romance.

The secret is like the art of seduction. Using the right automated technologies to bond with them. Building a relationship in an automated fashion, such that you know your prospect and your prospect feels safe enough to make a decision to trust you, and that trust then carries over to making a purchase of whatever it is that you're offering. And you can't shortcut this process and expect to get the same results.

ME-TO-YOU

This concept is as simple as it is ignorable. It means you speak directly to your customer as a real person on a one-on-one basis. "Me-to-you" means you don't speak in glowing, holier than thou terms. Be yourself. Talk to them as you would a close friend. Speak in a direct person-to-person conversational way, just like you and a good buddy or a close girlfriend are sitting down, one-on-one, catching up on the latest gossip.

Don't start out, "It's my pleasure to introduce to you blah, blah, blah." *Boring!*

You've already lost 'em and you'll never get 'em back. Instead, try this type of an approach: "Hey, I've got a hot tip for you. I've got to get you up to speed with what's going on."

Don't be afraid to use lots of slang for whatever is appropriate for the target market niche you're working in. You want to speak to people in their language, how they normally talk with their friends.

That's bonding.

However they speak, use that language when you communicate with them. You want to speak to them. That's the one-on-one, me-to-you bonding.

One of the biggest traps people get stuck in that creates dull, saleless marketing is they think they have to sell everyone and appeal to everyone with everything they say . . . so they dilute the message in trying to make it appeal to everyone by speaking in large generalities that have no real meaning or sales bite to them.

The way to stay out of this trap is to mentally pick one person who is your ideal prospect, and pretend you're speaking directly to just that one person. It's just the two of you . . . just you guys having a private, confidential conversation. See, you want them to bond with you and feel a connection with you as a person as opposed to a company.

I can't tell you how many times I see marketing (well, I shouldn't even call it marketing) that is signed by the "Customer Service Staff" or the "Customer Service Department." That just sucks! You do not want to alienate your customers or prospects by speaking to them as a giant, faceless, professional, high-on-the-hill company gracing the low-level peons, as most companies unknowingly do in their communications. Your communications should always come from a real person so the customer/prospect has a name to associate with the mental image she's already created in her head about you.

Just like the time you're spending with me here in these pages . . . I'm doing my absolute best to speak directly to you from my heart in a "me-to-you" way.

You wouldn't want me to sit here and give you boring textbook theory like in a classroom, like in college. You want to know: What's the scoop? Give me the skinny. Give me the straight deal. Tell it to me. Don't pull any punches. Don't sugarcoat it. Just make it the bottom line stuff, *and talk to me like a real person.* And that's exactly what we're doing together here.

See, I'm well aware that if I do a good job of bonding with you and giving you everything I can in my oh so "ShafMan Way" here, then in addition to the kinship you'll feel with me, hopefully you'll want to do business with me in the future by buying one of my products or services. Obviously, you'll buy more if you feel you got good value and fit well with my style. That's all because of the relationship we've started to form here.

And that's what you want in your communications with your customers and prospects.

Yes, you want *massive* numbers of people in your databases, but don't ever get caught in the trap of trying to communicate me-to-*everyone*. It's *not* me to a thousand of you, or ten thousand of you, or a million of you. *Each prospect, each person has got to feel that you are talking straight to them . . . one-on-one, me-to-you.*

This is the key to creating those hyperresponsive response rates we discussed earlier that are so different from mainstream, corporate results where a mail campaign is lucky to pull in a fraction of a percent of a percent of a percent results in response rates. And they say marketing doesn't work (well, in a sense they are right—*their* marketing sure doesn't work).

See, when you establish the bond, then you can have successes where 10, 15, even 30 out of every 100 in your database actually respond and buy.

And that's the difference. It's me-to-you. It's a relationship. It's trust. It's the bond. It's a tight rapport. It's me-to-you and you-to-me. Person-to-person, buddy-to-buddy, girlfriend-to-girlfriend. One-on-one.

Get it?

FEED THEIR PASSIONS, MAKE 'EM ITCH: THE "OHOLIC" TRIGGER

Mark calls it finding a Thirsty Crowd. . . . I call it tapping an "oholic" market niche. It's exactly the same thing. The key is to find a big enough group of people who are what I call "oholic" about a subject. That is, they are passionate, irrational, and almost insatiable about their addiction toward the particular subject.

A picture is worth a thousand words. Unfortunately, I don't have a picture that gets the point across that I'm trying to make here, so let me give you some examples instead.

- Golfers are nutty about golf and will spend a fortune to feed that addiction (and, generally speaking, golfoholics have the money to spend to satisfy their irrational needs).
- NASCAR enthusiasts are a very passionate crowd.
- Expectant first-time parents are some of the craziest people on the planet (I know I bought everything *anybody* told me I needed to have when I was there).
- The home-based business, work-from-home biz-opp seekers are *very* passionate about becoming entrepreneurs and achieving the freedom they dream of (by the way, if you haven't figured it out already, I'm a home-based-business-oholic myself).

- Multilevel marketers (MLMers) are a crazy, passionate bunch of people.
- People looking to lose weight (I've bought into some of the most cockamamy concepts and ideas because I wanted to believe the pitch as true).
- People who want to learn how to cook.
- People who call psychic hotlines.
- Day traders in the stock market.
- *Girls Gone Wild* video buyers.

Get the idea? The list goes on and on. In fact, we all have different areas of our lives and different subjects that we are "oholic" about.

My point here is that after you select the right "oholics" you must then arouse their passions and craziness about the subject. *Talk to their emotions about it. . . . Stir them up.*

See, if you've targeted the right "oholic" crowd you know they have certain passions, certain tendencies, and certain ways of thinking, and that's invaluable when you get to the bonding process. Knowing these things about the marketplace you are targeting allows you to create that bond. *It's about speaking their language.* And if you don't know their language you'd better learn it fast if you're serious about building a successful business in that niche, because, just like being part of the in-group in school, you will be immediately shunned by the people in the group if you don't truly belong.

I know this dates me, but did you ever see *Stir Crazy* with Richard Pryor and Gene Wilder? They end up going to jail with some very hard-core criminals. On the way in to the cells with all these killers sizing them up and checking out their butts, they are doing their best to fit in and be just like the killers by bebopping off-beat and saying "That's right, we bad, we bad."

You don't want to wind up standing out like that when you communicate with your marketplace. Just like the hard-core killers in *Stir Crazy*, your "oholics" will see right through your act and you'll fail.

THE BONDING POWER OF MEMBERSHIP, FRATERNITIES, AND SORORITIES

To create the bond fast, you've got to establish a common ground with your prospects and customers. And that means that you don't lecture to them, you don't talk down to them. You talk as we discussed, me-to-you, *conversationally.* And you do it in a way that's got personality and isn't dry. You do it in a way that puts you on common ground.

Why are sororities and fraternities so popular, and the desire to be a part of them so strong? It's because when you are a frat brother or a sorority sister you're a part of the in-group. You're accepted. You know something the rest of the world doesn't. You have friends who instantly understand you because you're all part of the same in crowd.

You want to create that environment where your prospect, where your customer, where your friend is on common ground. They get to join your fraternity or sorority (and they probably won't have to streak naked through campus singing "jingle bells" and "I'm a Little Teapot" to join your club . . . or will they?)

Anyway.

Now here's an important distinction that you must understand. Before you can take them where you want them to go, you first must meet them where they are. Therefore the common ground you meet them on is *theirs*, not yours. See, the shortcut to bonding is meeting them where they're at, bond with them where they're at. Talk to them on their level and then you have the opportunity to direct them. In hypnosis it's called pacing and picking up the pace. You match up with them and walk in the same direction they are walking and at the same pace they are walking. Then you have the opportunity to change the direction slightly and speed up or slow

153

down the pace. See the correlation? You first have to meet them where they are in order to take them to where you want them to go.

That's where the bond, the creation of the relationship happens. This can happen very quickly, or it can occur over time. It depends on the individual.

Generally speaking, there is a way to bond instantly, with every single person, right off the bat; but it involves molding yourself to that individual. If you're speaking in person with them, you can kind of pick up on what their personality type is . . . and figure out how to bond with them immediately. To meet them where they are, talk on their level so that they feel comfortable. *The instant you are like them, they feel that you're listening to them, and since you are like them, you have to be smart and know what you're talking about because to admit otherwise would be to admit to themselves that they are not smart.*

When you do this effectively, they're going to like you *because you are them.* Then the connection happens automatically. The difficulty comes in when you're doing it in an automated fashion, in print, in systems, because it takes time to bond. Because there are different personality types, there are different types of people and you can't mold your communication to the individual because you aren't sitting with them.

But there is a way to simulate that conversation with them: *have it with yourself first.* Think about what the prospect would be thinking, the questions they would ask, the objections they would have if they were there with you in person. Get that conversation down on paper. Now here's a shortcut for people who don't like to write or don't think they can. Speak into a tape recorder and then have it transcribed. It's really that simple. I do it all the time. As a matter of fact, what you are reading right now was first dictated into my handy digital recorder. As I was driving, ideas popped into my mind about what I wanted to share with you here. So I grabbed my little handy-dandy microrecorder and spoke into it just as if I was speaking to you face-to-face.

Then I had it transcribed. Now as I'm going back through it, I'm editing it, tightening it up, and adding additional ideas that come to mind, triggered by originally tape-recorded thoughts. See, it doesn't have to be hard or take a long time.

So when you don't have the luxury of sitting down in front of your prospect, you have to kind of take your best shot and then continue to build the bond over time. That's why you have some people who buy right off the bat, immediately, and it's also why you'll have people who take 10 times longer before they purchase. It takes a continual effort to build that relationship when you are in an automated fashion because you are kind of building the system for the masses. *But the good news is that once you set up these systems, you never have to touch them again. They just continue to work and do the bonding and selling job for you while you sleep, vacation, or are creating your next project!*

Another often-overlooked benefit of putting these automated systems in place is that although when you are speaking in person you can adapt to the individual immediately, you can't talk to massive numbers of people. You are limited by how many people you can sit down with and how many times you can give your presentation face-to-face. You can talk to only so many people in a day, in a week, in a month, and in a year. With an automated system, you can touch more people in a day than you could in an entire year of face-to-face contact. So, you're giving up some immediate ability to bond in exchange for the long-term effect, and I think you'll find that an automated system greatly outweighs the in-person approach, where you've got to do the manual labor, you've got to do the physical work.

PEOPLE WANT WHAT THEY CAN'T HAVE

Some of you may have read my training manual called *How To Make People Stand in Line and Beg to Join Your Network.* It's all about "posture power," as I call it, the ability to turn the tables and get your prospects coming to you.

The way that this is done is just the basic raw human psychology side of it, which is that *people want what they can't have*. People love the things that they can't have, especially in the United States. For some reason, and I don't know what it is, you tell somebody they can't do something, and all of a sudden they have to prove you wrong.

Use this to your advantage.

It's an interesting dynamic. You've got to use it gingerly. You can't slap them in the face with it. *You have to say things in a subtle fashion that makes them prove it to you*. For example, one of the techniques is "I can't promise you anything." The prospect mentally translates this to "I've got the greatest thing in the world, but I can't promise you that I'm going to be able to help you out with this. If you give me a call, I'll try to get to you, but, hey, please be patient with me because there are 3,762 people who want my attention this month." That's a subtle way of saying that you're extremely popular, and you're not sure if you want them. *All of a sudden you're hard to get and they'd be lucky to have you, and the thought of you turning them down is unacceptable.*

Connected with this concept is that we all get tired of what we have right now. It becomes old news and we naturally want to move on to bigger and better things. What's the next goal we want to achieve because we are unsatisfied with what is now?

Let's say you've always wanted a particular car, or to live in a particular area, or to get a new job. Nothing is more important, and you have made that your focal point. Finally you accomplish it. It sure does feel great . . . for a period of time. But sooner or later, you likely will get tired of that particular situation. It no longer holds the same intrigue. This phenomenon is a first cousin to the concept that people want what they can't have. *People get tired of what they do have and start to aspire to the things that they don't have, and therefore is kind of the circle that goes back into what you can't have you want. It's an insatiable need that makes the economy go around.*

I forget who said it. I think it was Paul Zane Pilsner, an award-winning economist, who talked about this principle. The example he used was cars. Carmakers originally thought that if they were to make cars that lasted forever and had more quality to them, they would eventually be put out of business because people would not buy cars anymore when one would last 10 to 20 years. But in fact, this is not at all the case. *What they found out is that the inborn human desire inside all of us is that we always want more.*

Once we get to a certain level, we're no longer satisfied at that level. We want more, we want something different, we want new, we want excitement. We want to continue to grow. That's also why, if you think about it, people get tired of their mates. Because they haven't kept it fresh, they haven't kept it alive, so they trade 'em in.

It works the same way with cars, houses, jobs, boats, electronics, and really anything else you can think of. Once the excitement and the newness rub off, we want the next bigger and better model.

Think about it in your own life, I know that's true for me. When I turned 20, I wanted a brand-new Ford Explorer. More than anything else I wanted that Ford Explorer. When finally I got it, I was so happy. And the joy, excitement, and enthusiasm for it stayed strong for two to three years. Then I started getting bored with it because I had gotten excited by other potential vehicles and I found myself saying, "I need something new. . . . I need something better." Then I went through the same routine when I bought my Lexus. See, the Lexus is a good luxury car, but I "needed" a rugged, beach fun mobile in addition to the Lexus. So I bought a red Jeep for weekend playtime. Now, as I write this, I've got my eyes on a hot Viper (I mean, I "need" that to complete me. I've got the Lexus for luxury, I've got the Jeep for fun in the sun. Now I need the Viper for speed and sport). By the time you read this I'll probably have bought it, and, who knows, maybe I'll even be starting to grow tired of that (although I can't imagine how I'd ever get tired of it. Then again I said that about the Explorer, the Lexus, and the Jeep, too. . . . Hmmm).

So what's the point of telling you this? It's *not* to show off. No, it's to point out that the behavior I just gave you the example of is inherent in every human being on the planet to varying degrees with regard to the subjects that they are passionate about, be it the next self-help book, the next novel, the next house, the next pet, the next trick they teach their dog, the next thing they do to improve their garden, or the next child they have. It's human nature and it's inside us all, and a smart entrepreneur, like you, knows to use it to your advantage.

See, our inborn desires are really insatiable. They continue to grow. And the beauty is that by satisfying your "oholic" buyers' insatiable needs for more and more and more, you give them exactly what they want, thus making them happy and at the same time you get rich so you can continue to buy more and bigger things you are "oholic" about. It creates the wealth that you need so you can satisfy *your* insatiable need and thirst for things, while satisfying the same for your customers in the process. Win-win.

It's this core concept that makes the hyperresponsive situation we discussed earlier even possible.

When you tap and harness this fundamental human nature principle, it creates the environment where you increase the lifetime value of every customer by getting them to buy from you more frequently and spend more on each transaction. And you provide a service at the same time to your people. Your people realize that they are insatiable. They are going to continue to want more and thirst for more in the areas that they're interested in.

They are going to satisfy that need somehow. If you don't satisfy it, they will go elsewhere to get their itch scratched. (Just ask a golfoholic. They'll continue to purchase anything, from anyone, that they perceive will help them. But if you aren't there with the answers, they'll go elsewhere to find them.)

So you just need to make sure that you're the one who delivers, who's there first to satisfy them the next time they get the itch. Then you're the one who continues to prosper as a result. If you make them bond to you, and you remind them that they itch and that you have the cure, they will almost force themselves into upgrading with you to the next level.

An extremely powerful concept to be sure.

THE GRASS IS *ALWAYS* GREENER

The grass is always greener on the other side of the fence is another closely related family member to people want what they can't have. Most people tend to want what they can't have, *and* for some reason they kinda assume that if they already have something, that it really can't be all that good. Unfortunately (or fortunately depending on how you look at it), we are a nation of people who want what they can't have and aren't satisfied with what they do have.

It's human nature to be in a state of *continual unrest*.

(On a personal note, I think the secret is to be happy where you're at, but to always have the aspiration for more so you keep growing, keep moving toward the attainment of your goals, and keep yourself alive and focused and passionate about life and its gifts!). . . . Oh, hey, did you notice I snuck in another little direct bonding personal communication to you just now?

When you are happy with what is, you're naturally at ease. But the funny thing is, when you're truly happy with where you are it opens the door for you to strive for more and really see those dreams come true instead of getting depressed when empty wishes aren't granted. See, when you aren't happy with what is in the moment, the chances are you are in a negative, desperate state of mind. This means that usually our judgment is controlled by fear (avoiding the pain of the present circumstances) instead of making decisions out of your vision for what you want to happen.

So this grass is greener syndrome is actually good, when used properly. It keeps you in growth mode and activity. There's always more that you can accomplish, always greater heights you can reach for. But also stop and smell the roses at the same time, because what's the point of making all this money if you're not enjoying where you're at when you're there. It's pointless, and you'll find that money solves a lot of things, but it doesn't create happiness; that comes from within.

A lot of people look at money and say, "When I make $XX amount of money, then I'll be happy." The problem is that money, possessions, status in life, relationships, and so on can't make you happy. Those are all things outside of yourself, while happiness comes from within.

I can hear you now. You are probably arguing with me: "Yeah, yeah, yeah, I've heard that all before. I don't buy it. It's easy for you to say that, Joshua—you're already rich."

Well, I can tell you this: As soon as you have some money, it *will* be very exciting, and you'll experience what I'm talking about firsthand. For me, it took about two years to come down off that high and realize that, hey, ya know, this has been great and I've enjoyed it, but this isn't what drives me anymore. Now I want do what feeds me spiritually, what feeds my personality, what gets me going with excitement that doing the project itself gets me ripping back the bedcovers, raring to go because I'm so amped up about it. *That's* what drives me these days, *not* the money. The money does come (and usually in much bigger amounts), but, believe it or not, it is a by-product of that mind-set, not the end in and of itself.

See, making money has everything to do with your mindset, with how you manage the internal mind conversations you have with yourself about it. Now I don't want to get too spooky with metaphysics here and get really off track, but I just want to put that out there, and there are some great books that you can read on the subject and really get an understanding. The first book that I would recommend to you very highly is the classic *Think and Grow Rich* by Napoleon Hill. Awesome book! I'd also recommend *Psycho Cybernetics* by Maxwell Maltz (Pocket Books, 1989).

Those are two excellent books to get you started and get you pointed in the right direction. So, as you start building your NPOD and start creating the wealth, you don't lose it all because your internal mind-set is off.

BE OPINIONATED . . . BE BOLD . . . BE AN OUTSPOKEN STRAIGHT TALKER . . . BE YOURSELF . . . LET PEOPLE KNOW YOU PERSONALLY . . . BUT . . . *NEVER EVER* BE BORING!

The next item that we're going to discuss in creating the bond and building hyperresponsives into your database is the concept of being *opinionated.*

That's right, you want to stand out as different. You want to slap people upside the head to get their attention so you have the opportunity to actually present something to them. But besides the shock value of being opinionated to gain attention, you want to use it as a way to bond with the customer. See, people tend to love (or hate) people who speak their minds on particular subjects. And, believe it or not, you don't care which it is, love or hate. If they love you, they will hang on your every word and agree with you, and therefore the relationship bond deepens. If they hate you, they will opt to leave you, which is exactly what you want because they weren't going to buy from you anyway. (You'll be well advised to get rid of the whiners who dislike you early on, as you aren't marketing to them. You're marketing to those who will buy from you. They are the people you're working for, not the other way around.)

So make a point, give your opinion straight from your heart, and be outspoken about it. Don't apologize for your opinion. Be bold about it. See, most people wish that their lives were more interesting and wish they had the guts to speak their minds. When they come across someone who has the guts to say what they are feeling, you become their hero. You are their champion. They wish they were you. Somehow listening to someone go off on a rant on a subject you're interested in is funny and exciting and has you nodding your head in agreement, which leads to a deeper bond. Opinionated people—you either love them or hate them, but you tune in to see what they're saying.

Case in point is Howard Stern. You either love him or hate him. Want to hear something amazing about that? His people have done studies on how long people listen to his show and why. They report that the average listener who loves him listens for something like an hour, and when asked how come they listen, the most common answer was "to see what he's going to say next." At the other end of the spectrum you have the people who hate Stern. The average person who hates him listens to his show for something like three hours, and when asked why they tune in, the most common answer again was "to see what he's going to say next."

Hmmm . . . ain't that a honker?

Think about what that means. People who hate him listen three times longer than those who like him. I'd say that Stern's opinionated approach works gangbusters. I mean, consider the fact that he gets paid based on ratings, and his ratings are determined by how many people listen and for how long. The more people he draws, the more they can charge advertisers to advertise on his show, which is what drives his entire success. Interesting—the people who hate him are actually making him rich.

If nothing else, Stern is very opinionated and very controversial. Being opinionated works wonders. People wish they could be that outspoken, that direct, that blunt. *They cry out for that freshness in their lives.*

Now, I'm *not* saying you should become a Howard Stern knockoff. No, I'm not. What I *am* saying is to take the concepts that he uses to make himself as successful as he is. Because regardless of if you love him or hate him, you've got to understand and respect the fact that he's a pretty intuitive marketer. *He knows what the public wants. When he's on the radio, he does some of the same thing we're talking about. He speaks to people kind of on a one-on-one basis. You feel like he's one of the guys, like he's your bud.*

The world is filled with people who are crying out for leadership and direction. They want to be told what to do. You want to be controversial in your own way. You want to be opinionated. But you want to be in a way that has a little twist to it, that isn't too condescending. Also, you'll find that *people really respect that straightforward, bottom-line, not sugarcoated approach, just kind of telling it like it is.* Just like using humor, you've got to be careful with how you use it. But it's too big, too important, too powerful a tool to not use it in some degree in your marketing efforts.

HOW TO GET THEM TO CALL THEMSELVES AN IDIOT

Here's a little trick that you can use that will serve you well, so always keep it in mind with all your marketing-related projects. You never want to talk down to your customers and/or prospects when you're trying to illustrate a point. Doing so will kill the bonding and relationship-building process you're trying to create.

Here's what you do instead (this works wonders). *Tell them a story and use yourself as the idiot.* Or tell them a story where someone else is the idiot. But don't ever make them the idiot by talking down to them.

Let me make this clearer. Let's say you want your prospects to understand the importance of taking action in their lives and

163

that procrastination will make them go broke and lose their families. If you say, "Hey, you idiot, you're never going to get anywhere in life if you don't do X, Y, and Z, if you don't get things done immediately, if you don't get up off your ass," they are going to mentally say "screw you," because it's like mom and dad lecturing them.

So how do you get them to do X, Y, and Z immediately with the same kind of impact and conviction? Simple. You could say something like, "I remember a time when I did X, Y, and Z, and I couldn't get up off my ass, and it really cost me greatly in this way, this way, and that way" and so on.

You always put it back on you in the form of a story so they get the point by seeing what happened to you. By calling yourself an idiot you take the confrontational pressure off, but the message still hits home. This is because what the listener, what the reader, what the person you are talking to will automatically do is put themselves in your shoes and see themselves doing what you did if they aren't smart enough to take your advice now.

So you've accomplished what you set out to do, which is telling them don't put it off, get up off your butt, and get it done instead of being lazy. In reality, you've told them it in a much more powerful way than just saying it directly because you told them a story about you when you got caught up in a similar situation. *So now they've got the message, but it hasn't been smacked upside their head directly.*

But there is an additional subtle thing you end up doing when you use this technique. When you tell your story with you as the idiot, you really get them saying to themselves, *"Glad that wasn't me. I don't want that to happen to me. I don't ever want to be the idiot he was."* Now as soon as they say that, you got 'em because now they *have* to follow your advice, because if they don't, they end up calling themselves the idiot! Do you see how powerful this is?

Now, this leads me to the next subject, which is closely related.

"IF *I* TELL THEM, IT'S AUTOMATICALLY *SUSPECT*... BUT IF I GET *THEM* TO TELL IT TO ME, THEY'LL FIGHT FOR IT AND AUTOMATICALLY ACCEPT IT AS *FACT!*"

I forget who said it first, but I think it was Tom Hopkins, a famous sales trainer, who said, "If I tell them, they doubt me. If *they tell me*, it's a fact." So building on our story technique from the prior section, if you make an assertion and expect them to just take your word for it, you'll die an ugly marketing death. Never just make a statement and expect them to take it at face value. You're the enemy trying to get some of their hard-earned money. You are not to be trusted and therefore they will automatically resist you.

But if you use third party stories, me-too stories, to meet them where they are by asking the right questions, you can create an atmosphere where you bring it out of them. Then the statement comes from them. They said it. It's their idea, and anything they say is immediately accepted as fact. After all, they said it!

Most people don't understand this and therefore don't bother to learn how to bond with their customers. This leads to the need to continually go after and try to bring in new business, instead of getting more business from the customers you already have. So, just like almost everything in our disposable society today, *the customer ends up getting discarded after only one use.* One time and you're done . . . you're off to look for another prospect to sell one time and discard. That's absolutely ludicrous, ridiculous, and leaves so much effort that you've just spent your time, money, aggravation, heartbreak, to acquire that first customer and get them to trust you enough to purchase from you the first time. After you get the customer is when the fun and work should really begin. That's where all the money is! To not service and sell that customer multiple times in the future is to leave 80 to 90 percent of the profits on the table.

Do *not* let this be you!

165

You want to sell the same person multiple products and services, because now they believe and trust you as demonstrated by the fact that they have spent money with you. That's the whole reason why you are going through this "blood brothers" bonding process.

NO ONE HAS EVER *WON* AN ARGUMENT!

Think about this for a moment: Nobody ever wins an argument. *Period.* I mean anytime you go head-to-head and aggressively (or even softly) try to convince someone they are wrong, both parties always lose. If you don't make yourself the idiot as we discussed earlier, then even if the other person says "You're right" usually it's because they just want to stop arguing. The person who says "Okay" to end it ends up walking away from the conversation feeling they are right and you are wrong anyway, regardless of what they say. They almost have to—their ego is hurt unless they defend their position. Now they're arguing just to be right, which is the hardest thing to overcome because they will irrationally defend their position to the death, no matter how irrational it may be.

Have you ever had this happen in your life? Has there ever been a time when you've been arguing with someone and said to yourself, "Screw it, this just ain't worth my energy and aggravation to continue arguing about this. I'm just going to shut up now." I bet the other person thought "Ah, I won." But, actually they haven't won.

Why? Because, first, you've shut down to anything they say from that point forward and you aren't listening anymore. Second, and more important, you're thinking, "What a jerk this person is. I'm not going to pay any attention to what he's saying anyway." Then you start thinking about things you've got to do later and anything but the conversation. They've lost you, right? So, no matter how well-meaning their message may be, you're over it and them and have tuned them out.

166

Not only have you tuned them out, but they've now created a situation with you where you *dislike* them. This person goes away thinking that they've won the argument—but they haven't. Neither have you, because perhaps this person had something valuable to say, but you missed out on it because of the way you guys were arguing about it. So that's why nobody wins.

This happens a lot in marketing situations—only not quite so obviously (if you think about it and keep on the lookout for it, you'll start to see the crossover applications).

"PEOPLE WILL WORK FOR MONEY, BUT THEY WILL DIE FOR A RIBBON!"

* Recognition * Recognition * Recognition *

Remember that everyone thinks in terms of their own selfish self-interests. In their minds they are the most important person in the world, or at least the most important person in *their* world. See, everyone longs to feel special, to be recognized. This deep, inborn need is in all of us to a greater or lesser degree. Why? Well, in life we don't get the recognition we feel we deserve; often the things we feel we should be recognized for go unnoticed or ignored. Everybody wants to feel special. Everybody *is* special.

Yet nobody gets the respect that they feel they are entitled to. *At least they don't feel that way.* It's an inborn craving. It's similar in principle to what we talked about earlier—people want what they can't have and people aren't satisfied with what they do have. Well, this is a cousin to that. I don't know why we are this way. We tend to be insecure beings, and as such we feel that we are not given the respect that we deserve. We are not given the admiration that we are entitled to.

It's an inborn craving or a gap, if you will, and that's why there's a saying that people will go to work for money, but they'll die for a ribbon, meaning that people will actually give their lives for recognition. They'll die to satisfy that craving of being respected. We'll work harder for that than almost anything else. It's much more of a motivating force than pure money itself. And very often the actual dollars aren't what we want, anyway. What we think they can provide for us is the driving force, the true underlying motivator.

So, if we know that we're insecure beings, and we know that that trait is present in almost everyone on the planet (that we all crave respect and feel we deserve it, but also don't feel that we get enough of it), we can play to that and bridge the gap for them. We know the gap exists for them, and they definitely know it exists. By giving them the recognition that they deserve, you're now automatically creating more of a relationship and more bonding.

If you keep this in mind and tap it (along with all the other techniques we are discussing here), the bonding process becomes a snap. It's a killer relationship builder.

So how do you tap it? The possibilities are as unlimited as your imagination. First of all, think about how you'd like to be recognized. What makes you feel special? How do you know when you are being treated with the respect and VIP status you feel you've earned? Turn that into the bonding experience that your database subscribers will go through.

Here are some quick ideas to get your creative juices flowing: send them a birthday card, surprise them with a special personal phone call or present that you didn't tell them about when they purchased the first time, give them your autographed picture, give them an autographed picture of a movie star, recognize their efforts publicly to your other database members in your newsletter, and so on.

Make sure you really congratulate them sincerely from the heart. Thank them. Be sure that you tell them how much you appreciate them. They are important to you. I'm not talking about mere flattery. No, I mean recognizing them from a very genuine place of sincere gratitude so they get just how important they are to you personally.

After all, everybody in your database *is* critically important and does mean something to you. They are your assets. They allow you to achieve your goals and dreams—to live where you want to live, to drive what you want to drive. Let them know that you know that and are appreciative of it, and something very interesting happens. You're delivering major value to them by just recognizing them. It's about value-for-value exchange. It's not about them just giving you money. It's not about you sucking them dry. You're giving them value. You're giving them what they need. You're giving them that feeling of specialness. You're giving them different products and services that are valuable (of course), but feeding this desire inside them to be recognized is one of the most value-building things you can do for your people.

The bonding process happens when you overdeliver on the value they are expecting to receive—when the value you deliver is over and above the price they paid. There is no price tag that can be put on making people feel respected, recognized, and special, so if that's part of the value you deliver, the value you create for this customer has just gone up to an almost incalculable level and they will gladly pay you for it. You're giving them psychological income or psychological value, which is often perceived as having a much higher value than hard-value items. Keep this in mind, and you'll always be able to create money on demand for yourself.

Hey, a quick aside: The price you charge for a product or service shouldn't have anything to do with the hard costs to produce it. It should be based on the perceived value it creates for the person buying it. If you can create something that costs you a buck to produce, for example, but it creates $10,000 worth of value for that customer, does that product warrant a $500 price tag? I'd argue, "Yes." Have you created incredible value for them? If they can go out there and create $10,000 in value from something they paid $500 for, is that a good deal for them? Hell, yes, it's a good deal for them. And you do that all day long. I would. Tell me a way that I can write you a check for $500 and I get $10,000 back. Yep, I'm doing that. My attitude is how many checks for $500 can I write you? I couldn't care less about how much the actual product costs to produce . . . just show me my $10,000.

Well, the same thing applies to the concept here. Don't get caught up in the cost. So you say to yourself, well, it cost me only a buck and I'm selling it for $500—that's not right. It absolutely *is* right . . . if it delivers on its promises and your customers get value from it.

Now one of the best ways to show your customers/prospects the potential value your product/service/associate/and so on provides is with imagery. One of the ways that you can make your customers and prospects feel really, really, really special, and make them feel like they're the most important person in the world is by *painting a picture and putting them in the picture*. Make them experience what it's going to be like when a certain thing happens in life.

For example: Picture how your friends and neighbors and family will be shocked, stunned, and amazed as they see you quit your job because you're making more from doing this than working for a living. Think about how good you're gonna feel when you get your first business model set up and you start making yourself a few hundred extra dollars the first month and then next month you make a few hundred more. All of a sudden it's up to several thousand. Then out of nowhere you buy yourself that brand-new Beemer or Mercedes convertible that you've always lusted after. You don't tell anybody; you just pull up in the driveway, and you watch your neighbors come out of nowhere with, "Where'd you get that?" And all of a sudden they're looking at you with jealous, envious eyes, and wondering, "Wow, how'd she get that? How did he create that? He only works down at the Circle K."

How good are you going to feel when you overhear members of your family saying things like, "I had no idea she would be able to build a business all by herself." And if you have kids, how they will look up to you knowing that their mommy makes more than their daddy now. Think about how good that would feel.

Can you see how it puts you in the picture? It's almost like you're living it right now, and it makes you feel special and has you experiencing the recognition you crave and deserve. I know from personal experience it was (and still is) images like this that kept me striving for more. It's never really just the money.

You want to make sure that you paint those types of stories for your people. But more important, put them in the positive stories, so they actually experience themselves physically in the particular picture that you painted for them. That's part of the bonding process.

Believe it or not, that very act of creating that vision, of creating those positive feelings for them, has value. As we discussed, the more value you create for them, the more bonded they will be to you and the more they will be willing to spend money with you and your company. Well, let me tell you something: *just putting them in that picture creates value in and of itself.* You make them feel good, and that is valuable to them. You have just given them value for free.

So you give them the recognition they crave, and although they might not give you money back in exchange (yet) they have given you something much more important. They have increased their trust levels and are therefore getting more and more bonded to you as a blood brother who understands and respects them. They are giving you the gift of their openness to hear more . . . and now you're on your way to creating hyperresponsive buyers.

One technique I've used very effectively is with my newsletter. When I get e-mails from people I often will reprint their question and praise them for such a good question. Or if they've shared a story with me, I'll praise them for the story in my newsletter. I'll say something like "The other day I got an e-mail from John Jones and he brought up an excellent point that I didn't do a good enough job explaining last month, and he's right. And now I'm going to right that wrong."

See what I did there? Did you catch it?

Actually I've done two things: First, I've given John the recognition he deserves, patting him on the back so now he feels special and is personally more bonded to me. But much more importantly than that is what it did for me in terms of bonding me to the rest of the entire database, not just John. See, now when everyone else on my newsletter list gets that e-mail and reads about how great John is and how he got me to see how I could have done a better job, it makes me more human in their eyes because they see I really do interact with everyone, listen to them, and give them what they want. It also makes them want the same kind of recognition that John just got from me in front of thousands of people. Now when Suzie reads about John she's more active, more responsive in the process; and now she's probably going to send me an e-mail in hopes that I'll recognize her in my next little relationship-building session.

And the cycle of deepening the bond continues.

Does that make sense? Are you starting to understand how to use this properly? That's the key. People have the desire to be recognized and satisfied. Give it to them. Plus, in the online world it becomes so easy to personalize things with mail merge functions that it gets easier and easier to do this. Then if you write in the me-to-you fashion we talked about before they will feel like the e-mail is just for them. They won't feel like it's a broadcast fax/e-mail that is going out to thousands of people in your database. They'll feel like hey, he's talking straight to me. Are you listening to me, John? Are you listening to me, Suzie? That's what will come across to John and Suzie, and everyone you are communicating with. It will come across like you are speaking directly to them.

You know it's funny—I've gotten tons of e-mails over the years from people in my databases who actually felt obligated to respond to my e-mail to them (which in fact was part of a mass e-mailing). See, my e-mail felt to them as if I sat down and composed that e-mail and sent it just to them. And that is the secret that we're talking about here. These relationship-building things that you're discovering are what create that feeling and obligation in your database.

GIVE 'EM INSIDER INFORMATION

A very powerful way of making someone feel special, like they are the most important person in the world, is to let them in on a secret that you wouldn't tell just anyone—the kind of information that you would only share with someone you trust . . . coveted stuff that you wouldn't share ordinarily. When you give people this kind of trust (of course you have to tell them just how powerful the info is that you are sharing and tell a little story about how and why you don't usually share it and how you can't even believe you are going to do it now). You make them feel special, and you give them respect by giving them insider information. The idea, the feeling you want to create with them is: "Hey, pssstt . . . comeheeerr . . . closer. . . . Shhh, nobody knows this and I'm only telling you because I like you, but . . ." There's bonding power in this technique.

Can you see how this creates the fraternity, sorority, insiders-only club?

I can hear you now . . . "What if I don't know any secrets they'd be interested in? I don't know anything like that." Let me speak to that for a second because it isn't true. Stick with me here and I'll show you what I mean.

A secret is a secret only if you don't know it. If that sounds like a stupid, obvious statement, that's because you're right, it is. But just like hiding in plain sight makes you impossible to find, the power of things this obvious is almost always over-looked. Let me explain. See, every single one of us has specialized knowledge in areas that we are interested in that is not known by the general population.

Think about the information you have been discovering on these pages that I've put together for you. This stuff is all second nature to me. I do all this stuff automatically now. It sure isn't a secret to *me* anymore. But how many times in just the last few pages did you say to yourself, "Wow, I didn't know that" or "I never thought about it from that prospective before"? My guess is that it has been many times.

When I explain my methods and thought processes to you, I'm letting you in on many secrets that all add up to giving you the power to create money on demand anytime your little heart desires. Is that an insider secret? You betcha. Did I learn it? Yep. Can you? Of course. See, the combination of what I'm delivering to you here is unique. What I've created is unique. It's based on information that I've discovered from the mean business streets and from doing my homework and learning from other very smart businesspeople. My passion to learn it and teach it makes the process of compiling this actually fun for me.

So what are some secrets you possess? You've got a bunch of them if you think about it.

Maybe it's a way of getting superior service at a restaurant. It could be a designer brand of perfume that is undiscovered that's going to be big, but before it gets discovered it is completely underpriced so your customers can get a deal on it now. Maybe you figured out how to get great deals on plane tickets. Did you go through a divorce and figure out how to keep from getting screwed? Do you have a great recipe for brownies? Did your grandfather give you a piece of advice on his deathbed that you have used as a guiding principle that has served you well for many years? Do you know a great fishing spot where the fish just jump into the boat? Do you know how to talk to your kids so they clean up their room the first time you ask them to do it? Maybe you know how to shave 10 minutes off your workout, and have been getting better results since you discovered it. Perhaps your aunt from China gave you her remedy for colds that works so well you've never caught a cold since.

And here's something really interesting: Sometimes the secret is in the way you deliver the information to them. What I mean is they may have heard it before, but you have a unique way of presenting it or explaining it so that when they hear it again from you, this time they get it. That's a form of inside information.

The possibilities are endless. We all have and utilize tons of these secrets each day. We just don't realize how valuable they are and don't consider them "secret" because we know them and work with them every day. We take them for granted and don't realize how astonishing and shocking they are to people who don't know them. And most people do *not* know them and therefore they are insider, secret info.

Now, because you are building your business model in an area you personally are passionate about, discovering *new* insider tips, tricks, secrets, and unusual information is fun, quick, and easy. Here's how: Just do a little homework. Go to the library and bookstore and get online and research it a bit. In three to five days you can become an expert on almost any subject you choose. All sorts of information are available on every subject imaginable. I dare you to spend a few hours researching a topic you're interested in at the library or online and not come up with a list of little-known tidbits of information that you say to yourself, "Wow! I didn't know that. This is some good stuff." If you don't come up with a list of 30 to 50 secrets you discover from a short research session, then something's wrong.

It's not like you're looking for the cure for cancer. No, I'm talking about little-known twists that the majority of your "oholics" wouldn't know and would be interested in and benefit by knowing. If you'll just spend some time, you can quickly come up with a list of 10, 20, 30, 100, or more of these little gems that you can introduce as your "jealously guarded secrets."

Another technique is to remember somebody's name and to use their name. Do not overuse it, but use their name. People want to know that you remember them and you respect them. That type of connection is important in the bonding process. So how does that translate over? Well, it's very simple. Use the technologies to mail merge their names in the e-mail. When you send them an e-mail, use their names. Don't just say, "Dear friend." Say "Hey, Joshua, here's what's going on, man." "Man, it's been a long time since we've talked, John." You can mail merge that right in, and there it is.

BONDING IS AN EMOTIONAL PROCESS, NOT A LOGICAL ONE . . . SO GET PERSONAL!

Bonding is about connecting with people on a personal basis. That connection is an emotional one, not a logical one (we love the people we do because of our feelings for them, not because we will ourselves to—and the same thing applies here). It's an emotional decision to trust. It's an emotional decision to buy. You (and your prospects) may argue this point and tell me, "No, I buy based on the facts," but all sales are made on the emotional level first, and then we look for the logic and reason we need to support our decision.

Unfortunately, I don't have the time to debate this point with you and try to convince you I'm right (encyclopedias have been written on this subject). For now you'll have to trust that after the tens and tens of millions of dollars my marketing has created, I know what I'm talking about when it comes to this subject.

So, if bonding is an emotional process, you've got to get *personal* in your communications. I know this is 180 degrees opposite of what the mainstream says and what traditional common business protocol dictates. But I'm talking about teaching you how to create *un*common results—how to create hyperresponsives and increase the LTV of your customers way over any mainstream business could possibly imagine.

Most people try to take their personality *out* of their business communications. They write dry memos and academic, institutional marketing pieces without the slightest hint they are talking to real people with real feelings, up against real problems. The result? No bond is created . . . no repeat business . . . no feeling of obligation to buy from you out of loyalty.

And no Second Glass of water is sold.

What follows is an excerpt from one of my newsletters that illustrates exactly how I connect with people personally and let them into my life in a way that creates a bonded friendship. As you read this, think about how opposite this is from other newsletters and marketing pieces you have received.

Pay attention to how I use a personal connection as a way to warm up to the subject and create a little romance so the reader is open and ready to hear what I have to say next. Pay attention to the way I use curiosity to keep you reading and, of course, how real what I'm sharing is to me and therefore connects on a deep emotional level. Think about how this builds commitment to me personally with the database and creates that inner circle membership feel we are looking for. See how you start to know me on a very personal emotional level and how my willingness to share my personal life with you makes you feel special that I'm letting you in on this stuff.

> The casket was to my left. I was smack in the middle of a heart-wrenching eulogy in honor of the loving woman who nurtured and raised me. All of sudden some unplanned words of wisdom just leaped from my mouth. The message even surprised me. It was like God (or something outside me, anyway) was whispering in my ear. Somehow it was exactly what the 300-plus people at the funeral (including me) desperately needed to hear at that moment. It effortlessly poured from my heart.
>
> It was very powerful. I *know* this because almost every

one of those 300-plus people went out of their way to tell me so. But the most meaningful comment came from a successful entrepreneur and powerhouse speaker. She told me with moist eyes and a slight quaver in her voice that my message was the answer to a personal crisis she faced.

Let me tell you, it could not have come at a better time for me. You see, the past four months have been bittersweet, to say the least. Actually, they've been among the toughest, most challenging—yet most exciting, passionate, joy-filled (not to mention absolutely the most lucrative, bar none)—of my life. Here's just a sample of what I've experienced . . .

In the past four months I was lucky enough to marry the most fantastic woman in the whole world. The bitter part? A week before our wedding her mother died very un-expectedly (actually, this deepened the love and bond be-tween us more than I can ever explain). Then I got the long-awaited news I'm gonna be a daddy and had tears well up in my eyes as I heard his or her thundering heart-beat for the first time. I helplessly watched three grandpar-ents pass away . . . but built a deep connection and strong friendship with my father-in-law while helping him through the shock and grief of losing his wife. And in the midst of it all managed to squeeze a little business in between.

(That's an understatement. . . . Business has *never* been better or busier—which, as it turns out, is going to al-low a few subscribers (maybe you) a unique opportunity to cash in big time! I've got something up my sleeve that's so amazing—such an incredible technological and market-ing breakthrough—that it will make you more money than having the exclusive marketing rights for Viagra! This is *big* [pun intended]. More on this later.)

Life's like that, isn't it? It's a mixture of stress, joy, dis-appointment, and triumph. It's quite a paradox. Often what you think is something really bad turns out to be a blessing in disguise (if you look for the hidden benefit and let it unfold).

Whatever. It's probably time I got off my soapbox and got down to business. . . .

What's that you say? Before we shift gears, you want to know what I said at the funeral? Hold your horses. I'll get to it. But first, let's get into the meat of the matter for this issue. . . .

Now, let me ask you a few questions: Do you feel like you just got a slice of my life? Do you feel closer to me as a person after reading that little excerpt? Do you feel like you know me and as though I trusted you like a friend to share something that personal with you? Are you wanting to know what comes next and hanging on the next sentence? Did it feel like I was sharing it with just you, like we were sitting down over coffee and I was catching you up on things?

That's what building the bond is all about. When you ease into things this way, not only do you increase the trust level but you also get your customers' and prospects' undivided attention so you can introduce your Irresistible Offer to them from a place where they are sure to hear you and thereby increase the percentage of hyperresponsives you have in your database from 4 or 5 percent to 20 or 30 percent.

This type of communication does something else very powerful for you: It gets people to look forward to your communications just because they are coming from you.

And, that, my friend, is pure platinum!

When your customers and prospects are waiting with anticipation for the next communication from you (like an excited five-year-old looks forward to Christmas morning), selling the Second, Third, Fourth, Fifth, Sixth, Seventh, Eighth, Ninth, Tenth, Eleventh (and on and on and on.) Glass of water is a piece of cake.

You're Getting Thirsty . . . Veee-rrry Thiirrr-sssstyy

Tellman Knudson

Tellman Knudson is a world-leading expert on attention deficit/ hyperactivity disorder (ADHD), an ultramarathon runner, and a master hypnotist. He has been learning direct marketing over the past year to apply these marketing methods to his ADHD consulting practice.

You can learn more about Tellman at his web site at www.ADHD Secrets.com.

So, this is the advice that Mark is giving you, huh?

1. Create The Irresistible Offer.

2. Present it to a Thirsty Crowd.

3. Sell them a Second Glass.

He has a pretty strong argument, doesn't he? I thought he did, but I didn't see how I could apply it to my existing business (doing teleseminars) until I asked him about it on the phone one day.

You may have been following Mark Joyner closely for a while, and if you have, then you know his book *The Irresistible Offer* was published recently, and this one, *The Great Formula*, went to press just a few short months later. So what gives?

When Mark asked me to contribute a chapter to this fantastic work of marketing genius, I took a long, hard look at the past several months in my business. Before I agreed to tell you about my experience with Steps 2 and 3 of the formula, I had to make absolutely sure that I had some rock-solid examples of his concepts in practice.

Fortunately for everyone involved, I have earned thousands of extra, icing-on-the-cake dollars as a result of presenting my offers to a Thirsty Crowd and then selling them a Second Glass.

I remember the day when I was on the phone with Mark, and I was struck clean between the eyes with a great idea—and it involved the phone, of all things!

But, before I get into how I applied these principles after I met Mark, you are going to be *really* excited about how I applied them to my business *before* I met Mark. Check this out—you are going to be able to use this idea in whatever business you are in.

As a hypnotist and neuro-linguistic programming (NLP) practitioner, I help people to transform their lives by learning how to use their brains more effectively and to change their habits, thoughts, and actions—quickly, effectively, and permanently. When I began, earning $75 an hour (the most I'd ever made an hour at that time—hey, I was just out of college), I thought that I'd be rolling in the dough once I just got my business cards and brochures around town in strategic locations.

However, there was a small (but catastrophic) problem just waiting for me, right around the corner of my business plan. If you are in the business of working with people one-on-one or in small groups, you will immediately get what I am talking about here.

Picture this: Some guy trains as a hypnotist. He has amazing skill and is totally dedicated to his profession and helping people. He quits his day job to focus on building his business. After an initial surge of clients, things level off. Suddenly, he is having a hard time paying the bills.

The cupboards are bare, the fridge is all but empty—and there aren't even any Ramen Noodles left in the drawers. It's time to go out and buy a sandwich for lunch, I guess.

So, he goes to the closest deli and orders a BLT, a cup of

soup, and a cup of coffee. He sits down, and goes inside his own head to try to figure out how he is going to make this work. As he chews on the sandwich the stress continues to build—and the answers don't come by the time the meal is over. The grand total is less than $10. He goes to pay with his debit card (he cut up all of his credit cards a few months earlier because they just put him further into debt). That's when the hit below the belt comes.

Wham! The card gets rejected because he doesn't have $8.95 in his bank account. That hurts.

He manages to convince the owner of the deli that he will go get some cash from his apartment (and manages to borrow some cash from a friend) and gets his lunch paid for by the end of the day.

That is the day he decides that things have to change, and he'd better use some innovative thinking to drum up some business fast, or it will be time to go back and work at the Bread Factory.

Yeah, we both know who the guy was. It was me, just a few short years ago. But let me tell you about how I got myself into that situation—and how I managed to get out again. Here was the problem—or rather here were all the problems—with my business plan:

- I had no advertising money.
- I wasn't in regular contact with my past clients.
- I was earning $75 per client that I had, most of which went to paying rent for my office.
- I wasn't known in my area as a "master hypnotist" (yet).
- I needed immediate clients who wanted to obtain my services and hand me checks.
- My practice was in a rural, skeptical area of Vermont (still there!).

- The area I live in is generally on the low end of the economic bracket, and there is a high ratio of young people who aren't in college—meaning most of them don't have much money.

What was the solution? Here we go:

I knew that I needed people who were thirsty, right? A Thirsty Crowd. I also knew that the top three uses of hypnosis in the world were for weight loss, quitting smoking, and stress reduction. But I wanted to be focused on my area of specialty—attention deficit/hyperactivity disorder (see www.ADHD Secrets.com). So what did I do? Well, I noticed that no matter what, I would get weight-loss clients every week, even when I wasn't advertising that hypnosis could help with weight loss! So, even though it wasn't my first choice of interest, I decided to focus on weight loss first—because that was the hungriest crowd in reach.

(*Note:* If you are getting a certain type of client/customer that you don't advertise to directly, focus *all* of your energy on getting more of those types of customers *if* they are profitable.

So, I knew that I should focus on getting more weight-loss clients. But where would I find them? I already knew that hoping they'd find my brochures and come to me wasn't working well enough.

Well, I also knew that the vast majority of my clients at the time were women, and that women usually will seek out health solutions much more readily than men would—so I knew two things about the clients I was looking for. One, they were overweight, and two, they were women.

And I knew something else. I also knew that all of my clients had to be able to afford to pay me $75 a visit *and* be willing to spend this money in order to lose weight. This filters out a very high number of people who aren't willing to spend money to solve their problem. So, I narrowed my profile down to what would look like my perfect client.

Then, I sat down and brainstormed a list of places that my perfect clients would hang out at.

What places did I come up with?

- Fast-food restaurants.
- Grocery stores.
- Weight-loss clinics.
- Doctor's offices.
- Salons.
- Other alternative health centers.
- Gyms—specifically gyms geared toward overweight women.

So, these were my top choice locations. They all had paying customers who were women and who were overweight! How could I tap into their client base? Simple.

I came up with the idea of a mini-practice: I went to all of the weight-loss clinics, salons, alternative health centers, and women's gyms within an hour's drive of my home—and this was my pitch:

"If you have an empty room in your workplace at least one day per week, I will offer all of your customers a free session with me. If they come back for more, I will give you 33 percent of whatever I make. This is extra income that costs you nothing to make—and all you have to do is let your customers know that you will set up a free session for them with me if they would like to check it out."

Guess who said yes? *Everyone* who had a free room! I even got a mini-practice started up in a dental office! So, within a month, I had not one, but five hypnosis offices with client bases. They were in a women's gym, a dental office, an alternative health center, a weight-loss center, and my private office. That's the equivalent of five separate practices. I spent one day per week in each office, and the overflow for the weekend would go to my private office.

So, the first Thirsty Crowd in this scenario was the business owners who, of course, wanted to make more money. I offered them a way to make more money in their existing locations without having to invest any more time or money than they already were investing. How could they refuse? I sold them on my idea initially, and then I sold them a Second Glass by handing them checks at the end of each day. Once they started to benefit, they wanted me to start coming in more and more; so soon I wasn't there only one day a week!

The second Thirsty Crowd was the customers themselves. Let me tell you how this worked. When I started this concept up I was just charging people per visit—but I found that I had frequent no-shows. Also, people would often come in for only two paid visits, when they really needed to see me 5 to 10 times to make a long-term change with weight loss. Consequently, my clients were getting short-term results—they ended up gaining the weight back. So, I tried something new one day.

Usually, people would come in for their first visit, then would ask what their options were from there. I would overdeliver on that first visit, and always give people 90 minutes of my time instead of the one hour I promised. I would also record the session so they could take a tape or CD home to listen to over and over (and it had my name and phone number on the front so they could contact me easily). But at the end of the visit I would just suggest that they could make another appointment or call me if they wanted more. Some did; some didn't.

So, beginning on this day, I did something different. I began my sessions the usual way—overdelivering as always—but I offered the first session for free. And at end of the session I would tell them that they would get the best long-term results if they came in for 5 to 10 sessions. I said they could pay for one session at a time at $75 a pop—and if they did that for 10 sessions it would add up to $750. Or, I said, they could pay for a block of five sessions right now and get them for the price of four sessions. That would be only $300—and they could do it again at the end of their first block and save $150.

After that, about 80 percent of my free clients became paying clients—and 75 percent of them paid me $300 at the end of a *free session*. The best part is that anyone who paid in advance would always show up for their session because I told them that if they didn't give a minimum of 24 hours' notice, the session would be forfeit.

Then, I turned around and sold CD sets during their next session to people who wanted to get on the fast track to their goals.

Now, here is the thing. All of my sessions were top-notch and completely customized. If I had a free spot open after a client I was seeing, I wouldn't take the time off. I would see that client for 1 hour and 45 minutes. Or, if they had to go at the end of their session I would go out into the waiting room for the main office (dental, weight-loss clinic, or gym) and I would announce, "I just got an opening. The first person who is ready gets a free hypnosis session!"

Bam—I got swarmed by people and filled my appointment book for the next three weeks!

Oh, one more thing. If anyone *ever* asked for their money back, for any reason, I would always give it to them (fortunately this happened only twice in my career).

So, remember, here is the process I used.

1. I found out where my Thirsty Crowd was and went to them.

2. I gave them a sample and overdelivered.

3. I sold them a package of multiple sessions.

That's it. It changed my life. It didn't cost me a dime to put together (remember I was using other people's existing facilities and customer base—that meant no rent or advertising costs). Using this system, I filled my days with clients and my bank account with money. Then, I learned about working with groups . . . but that's another story for another day.

So, how do I use these methods today in my business as it exists now? The real answer is, I use them all the time, everywhere—but for now, I am just going to tell you about one little slice of my existing business, to keep it as simple as possible.

Let's get back to Mark Joyner and what I have learned from him in the past few months. See, these days most of my business happens online, where I can sell people products by the thousands, instead of one at a time.

I have learned a very important lesson. When you make a sale you aren't necessarily making money; as a matter of fact, you make a lot more sales if you start with a different type of exchange. Whenever you get someone to take a desired action, you are making a sale. You are selling your idea to someone in exchange for something.

It could be any type of exchange, but ultimately it is an exchange of value. That exchange can include time, money, or energy. Online, for many people, the first exchange happens when someone enters their name, their e-mail address, and sometimes their phone number in exchange for information they want—opting in. You can actually see this process in action on two different web sites. Check out www.ADHDSecrets.com or www.asktellman.com. When you go there, enter your information (name, e-mail, and phone number), so you can see step-by-step how this sales process works.

This is where the teleseminars I do now (seminars or classes that take place on the phone) come in, and how I benefit, in this case, by the offer of a Second Glass.

You should remember that, in the Past 12 months, I have become the top salesperson (or affiliate) for several programs through the use of teleseminars. As a matter of fact, my company alone has made over $700,000 in sales in the past eight months just through teleseminars—and the method I am about to share with you right now. Listen carefully, because the way I do this is not going to be what you think it is.

Here it is, the sales method that has added over $6,000 of

extra, automatic money to the sales I have made—just in the past three months:

As we have seen, the first sale that happens is when we have an exchange: You give me your contact info, and I give you information that you are interested in.

Now, say you put your name and e-mail in (you opt in)—then you get to a page where I make you an offer. (This, of course, would be The Irresistible Offer.) Say you decide to take me up on my offer, and you put in all your information and press "submit." The very next page you go to will be what is called the Thank You page. This is where the magic happens—because my Thank You page is quite different from your normal Thank You page.

At first it may not seem much different to you. But I want you to take a good look at what happens here. You are being given some very clear directions on what you need to do next, and they almost always look like this:

Step 1 is usually to go and confirm your subscription to the newsletter (this keeps your ear open to further communications—and sales opportunities—in the future).

Step 2 is to listen to the recording of a teleseminar (or to call in to a live teleseminar).

Step 3 is to "Do Your Homework." This is another call to action. It is asking you to go and do something else that will give you what you are looking for. It may be to sign up for something else, or it could be a link that brings you to a sales page where you buy something.

This third step, the "Do Your Homework" step, is the Second Glass.

Want to see an awesome example of how this works? Go to www.asktellman.com, and when you get through to the Thank You page, be sure to click on the homework link.

This one technique alone has made me more than $6,000 in the past three months—with minimal use. But remember, this was all *extra money*. These are all additional sales that I wouldn't have made otherwise. All I had to do was add an extra link to my Thank You page.

Now, this is where it gets powerful. What happens when you are selling people on something that they get charged for month after month? Yeah, you guessed it—you get checks in the mail month after month. But, you should realize, this is a challenge if you don't have your own monthly service. You have to think creatively.

Well, that's exactly what I did with this technique to make thousands of extra dollars every month, *and* make friends with people who would help to promote my products and services in the meantime.

Consider this: If that link on your Thank You page sells your customer on someone else's monthly product or service, then you win and they win and your customer wins.

Let me explain.

In business there are all sorts of ways to split the sales and profits. Remember earlier when I told you about how I offered 33 percent of my hypnosis sales to the different business owners I set up shop with? Well, that is the same process we are talking about here.

What happens if I recommend that someone go and use a special service that gives them the best way to put audio on their web site—and tell them they can get a $1 trial by going to my favorite audio web site? Well, the customer goes and gets a trial, then gets billed for continued use after the trial is over. They get a great service, the service provider gets a cut, and so do I—in the form of a check in the mail for as long as that person stays a customer.

But, you can do this all day long! What happens if you are selling someone a $1 trial to one service, but as a bonus they also get a trial to another complementary service? Well, the answer is simple. You get two checks every month instead of one *and* you don't have to provide the service or the customer support.

This is the power of The Great Formula.

I want to tell you one more *very* powerful way to use this concept before I wrap things up. This one is brand-new, and I mentioned it at the beginning of this chapter. Here is what we are doing now.

Remember what I told you about the Thank You page. The Thank You page is the equivalent of someone booking an appointment with you (because they just gave you their contact information and said they want to do business with you). If you run any type of business where people have to make an appointment or register to see you, then you can apply this idea.

Someone has taken your desired action (made an appointment, put in their name and e-mail, or made the first purchase). Now, you want to immediately give them what they are looking for, and give them a chance to buy something from you while they are waiting. Let me give you an example.

On several of my teleseminar registration forms, when you hit my Thank You page I may *not* give you a link to click. Instead I might give you immediate access to another teleseminar—except it is one that is recorded. That recorded teleseminar presents information that will be useful to you (and will sell you something at the end)—but won't conflict with the teleseminar that you are waiting for.

Now, how can you apply this if you are a dentist or a mechanic? It's simple. What if, when people call to make an appointment, you book their appointment and tell them to look in the mail tomorrow, because you are going to overnight them a special report about "The 7 Steps to a Sexy Smile and Saving Money on Your Next Trip to the Dentist" or "9 Ways to Double the Value of Your Vehicle and Save Thousands with Your Mechanic."

Well, I'll bet that they will read that special report before they come in to see you—and at the end of that report you tell them how they can get a subscription to your monthly "Sexy Smile and Dental Savings" report—and if they call your office to order in the next 24 hours you will give them half off the price of their subscription.

Bam! You just made a recurring sale before the person even comes in for their appointment. *Plus* it gives you a way of staying in constant contact with your paying customers. *And* they will thank you for it.

Not half bad, if you ask me.

Creating an Unending Wave of Win-Win-Win Promotions and Strategic Partnerships

Dr. Joe Rubino

Dr. Joe Rubino is an internationally recognized business and personal development trainer and best-selling author of eight books, which are available in 19 languages and in 48 countries. As an acclaimed speaker and course leader, he has impacted the lives of more than 500,000 people through personal and leadership development, teaching them to increase their productivity and live "values-based lives without regrets." He has also personally coached thousands of people to become successful in their traditional businesses and in the profession of network marketing. Dr. Rubino's vision is to help people to be their best and shift the paradigm around resignation—anyone can effect positive change in their own lives and in the lives of others if they believe they can."

To find out more about Dr. Joe Rubino's work, visit his web site at www.CenterForPersonalReinvention.com

Before I tell you my story, it is important that I share with you my self-declared life purpose: to impact the lives of 20 million people to be happy, abundant, and self-actualized—in short, to be the very best they can be. For, you see, although I like the money that comes from these brilliant marketing techniques as much as the next guy, it really goes beyond finances alone. It's about the ability to reach thousands, or perhaps even millions, who could not have been reached by traditional marketing alone.

By following Mark Joyner's Great Formula, I have been successful in introducing my books, CD and cassette albums, coaching services, courses, and keynote speaking to new individuals and companies. The formula all began with The Irresistible Offer. For my book *The 7 Step System to Building a $1,000,000 Network Marketing Dynasty* (John Wiley & Sons, 2005) my goal was to identify individuals who want to build a home-based business. We targeted network marketers as they are a ready-made Thirsty Crowd for my books on this topic. We also identified potential candidates who were not yet involved with a network marketing opportunity but might be open to considering alternative ways to generate income from home.

To get the word out about the book's launch, I partnered with about 45 people who mailed to about 1 million subscribers on their lists. These mailers were centers of influence, people who already have target markets likely to see a fit for my book topics. In other words, I looked for people who had Thirsty Crowds already lined up. I then created win-win-win offers to benefit the list owners (centers of influence), book buyers (Thirsty Crowd), and our company (providers of books, audio programs, courses, coaching, etc.), all the while creating extraordinary value for everyone involved. I found these centers of influence by contacting my friends involved in the network marketing profession, researching web sites via search engines, browsing through magazines, subscribing to pertinent e-zines, and other sources where experts in my book's subject area were featured. I asked them if they would be interested in a joint venture: They provide a bonus of interest to my book buyers (helping them expand their names list) and they agree to send the promotional offer to their list (helping me sell books).

On my very first attempt, with the help on these partners who agreed to mail my benefit-laden offer to their lists, my book reached number 25 on the Amazon best-seller list on April 15, 2005. As promised, each of my book buyers received a listing of approximately 30 bonuses of interest to network marketers. These gifts were provided by many of the centers of influence who also had agreed to mail the offer to their lists. Along with receiving the free gifts, these book buyers were invited to visit www.cprsuccess.com, sign up for my complimentary Center for Personal Reinvention newsletter "The Power to Succeed," and purchase additional books or audio programs from my web site (in return for receiving special discounts and additional free gifts).

As a secondary benefit of introducing these buyers (my Thirsty Crowd) to more information on how they can be more successful in building their businesses and more effective in influencing others with integrity through my books and tapes, 27 new clients contacted me for continuing personal coaching at the rate of $150 per hour. Sixteen also enrolled or expressed serious interest in my *Conversations for Success* Courses in Personal and Business Development for the tuition of $895 each. Not only did this generate revenue for me, but through these promotions, I have been able to influence the lives and business success of all these people whom I never would have met had it not been for the help of my friends in getting the word out about what I do. This method of using The Great Formula continues to enable me to reach more great people and have the opportunity to champion their lives.

Since this first promotional launch, we've beefed up our ability to collect data (grow our names list) and correspond with these people effectively (through a series of turnkey autoresponders, affiliate programs, and a state-of-the-art shopping cart we've put into place, www.wealthywork.com, which has been a true blessing!). In the next two weeks, with the rollout of my next book, *The Ultimate Guide to Network Marketing*, we are expanding on the formula by inviting more people (55) to offer more bonuses of value to our book buyers ($4,450 worth), mailing to more people (about 2 million), and then offering a Second Glass, which will consist of additional value-rich bundled offers of books, CDs, coaching, and courses, all intended to champion the Thirsty Crowd who by the very nature of our business will be more likely to achieve success and thereby introduce countless others who will also be thirsty to learn the secrets to success and fulfillment.

Passion and E-mail in The Great Formula

Andrew Fox

In 1999, Andrew Fox set up a safe-list web site with a business partner. The web site developed such a huge following that by the time they released their second web site, Gurumailer.com, Andrew and Laurence were earning up to $10,000 recurring monthly income within 10 days.

Andrew's success with his online businesses led him to be asked to speak at the Internet Super Conference in July 2002. At that time, he was a fresh-faced kid from Ireland, barely 21 years of age and the youngest speaker there, but already he was recognized and respected as an authority in online business and marketing.

Andrew then turned his talents to resale licenses. Over a two-year period he released four high-quality products with resale rights. With each new project, Andrew has carefully and consistently expanded his following and established a loyal repeat client list. The result of all this hard work is that whenever Andrew releases a new product, he can have full confidence that it's going to sell well, and that is truly a great achievement.

Andrew lives in Ireland, but spends a lot of time traveling over to the United States to attend Internet marketing conferences and find new promotional partners. If you would like to learn more about Andrew and his projects, please visit http://millionairesmegayacht.com /andrewlaunch.

1. What are the various ways people can identify and address crowds thirsty for their product?

Identifying Thirsty Crowds is really not as hard as you might think. I'll give you a few methods that work really well.

I always like to think of one word when sourcing out a new market:

Passion!

You got it. Passion is what makes people more motivated than any other factor in buying something. In many cases people trying to create a product focus too much on the "selling" aspect. Apply to people's emotions such as passion and combine that with fear of loss and you are in the middle of creating something very special.

Here's an example. Personally I'm a Ferrari enthusiast; I can't get enough of the damn things. I'm *passionate* about them.

Now if I find a web site selling a DVD collection of the top 10 Ferraris of all time I'm going to be interested. However, the way to sell to me is to write about how this DVD features things such as "The demon red Ferrari 355 versus the awesome V-8 sound of the Ferrari F40."

A picture is being painted in my mind via use of color "red" and sound "awesome V-8."

Use pictures and sounds to take over your readers' minds. Suck them in. You are telling a story but selling at the same time. This is a great technique and is a lot smoother than saying, "Buy my DVD."

Here's another rather strange example: Your dog gets so excited every time it sees a new guest it wets itself. Create a book on how to stop this problem. Use a headline like "At last, your solution to avoid cleaning up your dog's mishap every time he meets a new guest—no more embarrassment ever again!"

You are applying to an emotion of someone, and a very powerful one—embarrassment. Get into your prospect's head, create a picture, and provide the solution!

So when you want to find a Thirsty Crowd think of people's emotions and passions. It's what calls people to action every day without them even knowing it.

Another excellent way to identify a thirsty market is by looking at blogs online. The key is to look at the response a certain post gets. For example, one post could have five comments while another post has 50 comments from the same audience!

Do you see what I am getting at here?

See what people are responding to, what makes that topic so hot. A lot can be learned by gauging other people's actions and responses.

2. What are some cool ways you've done so in the past?

Well, part of my business is Internet marketing.

A way I've made money is by acquiring resale rights to a product that I can sell for a 100 percent profit. Let me quickly explain what I mean by this. Recently I purchased a resale license to a product for $1,997. I was then allowed to sell this product for $697 without paying anything to the author. To date I've sold around 100 copies of this course. I received $69,700 in sales for a single $1,997 investment. Not bad!

I thought to myself there must be a market of people who would love to acquire resale rights to products but not costing as much as $1,997.

I decided to offer resale rights to a product at $697. I selected this price to make it affordable to most people without making it too low and attract cheapskates.

The product was an instant success! A few years on I've released four resale products, the most recent being "Launch a Product." You can see details at www.ultimateresalelicenses .com/lap.

Because of the loyal following I have built up in the past two years for high-quality resale licenses, we sold out all 97 licenses very quickly, costing $697 each.

It's like money on demand! I keep providing high-quality resale licenses once, maybe twice a year, and I always have a steady customer base of repeat buyers, which we all know is the lifeblood of any business.

3. What are the various ways people can offer a Second Glass to their customers (after the initial sale—the back end, essentially)?

This is one of the *easiest* ways to dramatically boost your profits with no extra work. If you are not using it, then you are leaving a heap of money on the table.

Let's go back to the Ferrari example in the first section. Okay, I've decided to buy the DVD collection and have reached the order form.

"Order form" is another term for "time to explode your profits." Your prospects have decided to part with their hard-earned cash, so why not try to get them to order another item hassle free?

Let's imagine this.

We are on the Ferrari order form, and it's reminding us we are purchasing the DVD collection. But before we get to the section where we enter our credit card details there is a small box saying "Hey, as you are buying the Ferrari DVD collection would you be interested in adding a subscription to our Ferrari newsletter at 30 percent of normal price? Check this box if you wish to add this."

From past experience, I estimate anywhere from 20 to 60 percent of buyers will take the extra package. That's extra profits for simply changing one item on the web page. Does 30 minutes of work for a lifetime of profits sound good to you?

But there is still money to be made in the order process.

After customers order they will be taken to a page thanking them for their purchase.

A great way to earn additional revenue but not appear to be selling to the customer is by giving a free bonus.

The thing is this bonus can be something like "As a one-time offer you can have a three-month free subscription to our sister BMW magazine by clicking this box." Subscribers are not charged for the first three months but after that they start paying monthly.

So what started as a single DVD purchase can build into two extra subscriptions with no extra work on your part.

These techniques really blow your profits through the roof. Try them in your own business and see for yourself.

4. What are some cool ways you've done so in the past?

In April 2003 I created a web site called Gurumailer.com.

It was a safe-list web site. When you joined the service you could send your offer to the list but in exchange you had to receive offers from other members of the list.

However, the system was set up so you could send your offer only twice a month. The price was $27 monthly.

When you reached the order form there was an "Upgrade" membership option. Instead of the gold option at $27 a month you could take the platinum option, which allowed you to send your offer four times a month for $37 monthly.

We had around 60 percent of all customers take the upgraded option, which was incredible.

For example, 12 monthly payments at $27 = $324.

But for the upgraded option, 12 monthly payments at $37 = $444.

$444 − $324 = $120 extra profit per year per member.

Multiply that figure by 1,000 members and you have an extra $120,000 per year!

So in summary, if you are not offering you customer a Second Glass you are leaving a *lot* of profit on the table for no extra effort.

Well that's about it for now. I hope this information has been helpful to you as a reader.

If you want any more information about my products please go to

www.ultimatemarketinglicenses.com.

"What's the Secret to Completely Dominating Any Market within 180 Days?"

Brad Callen

Brad Callen is the owner and founder of Bryxen Software and began his online career in the "health and fitness" niche. Not many people are aware that "weight loss" and "lose weight" are two of the Internet's most competitive keywords. Brad achieved number one Google rankings for both these keywords, bringing in a flood of free search engine traffic to several of his web sites and beating out Fortune 500 companies with millions of dollars in advertising revenue!

Brad is also the owner of seoelite.com (SEO Elite), which, in less than one year, has become the number one ranked Clickbank.com product, and is one of the top two search engine optimization (SEO) products in the world.

To find more about Brad's work (he runs over 40 web sites), you can visit www.seoelite.com, www.linkmetro.com, www.seoelite.com/ 7DaysToMassiveWebsiteTraffic.htm, and www.keywordelite.com.

In the next few pages, I'm going to present you with a simple example that I've used to dominate a niche market in 180 days. You'll learn how I took a product from nonexistence to completely dominating the industry in a matter of six short months. I'll show you exactly how I discovered the needs of a Thirsty Crowd, and created a product to satisfy that thirst. I'll then show you a few methods I used to offer them a Second Glass, to maximize the value gained from each customer.

Without further ado, let's begin.

Before you create any product, you should have your

mind made up that you will stop at nothing to make your product truly great. This simple mind-set is very important. The better your product, the more you will sell and the less money you will have to spend on advertising. People (your customers) will willingly advertise for you without you even knowing they're doing it. Word of mouth is the greatest form of advertisement one can have.

Now, let me give you an example of what I'm talking about. Around August of 2004, I released a software product called "Link Proctor." Ever heard of it? Probably not. The software's sole purpose was to help users manage their links pages (the web pages that contain links to other web sites). The software sold for $67. At that time, I was entering a market in which I had no real contacts that I could get to promote my product. Here I was, completely new to the industry. I had created a simple little tool that solved a common problem for this market and needed to market it to the world, but I had no real connections to the part of the world that would be interested. This is obviously a very big problem.

Or is it? Here's the story.

I did a little research and found several of the most popular search engine optimization forums, which is the type of market that, I thought, would want my product. This was my Thirsty Crowd, the crowd with the problem that I knew I had the exact solution for. I knew this because I had spent several weeks earlier monitoring these forums, looking for commonly asked questions/problems that no one seemed to have a good solution for. Monitoring forums is an excellent way to find a Thirsty Crowd.

Next, I selected one of the three forums I had found, and purchased a skyscraper banner ad on the web site. The banner ad was very expensive, but I knew that many targeted prospects would see the ad, click the banner, and possibly purchase. I didn't care if I lost money the first several months. As long as I could build a customer base, I knew I would eventually begin making money, regardless of how small a base I generated from this ad.

I actually ended up losing money the first month. About two months went by. I made some sales—not a lot, but enough to get started. Now that I had a small customer base, I knew I had to do something to get these people talking. Creating a buzz is what you should strive to do with any product you create. In my mind, a customer base means having my own private sales force working for me, 24 hours a day, 7 days a week, for free. Keep in mind the majority of my customers were people that were very active in the forum I was advertising on. Forum advertising is one of the best ways to sell a product. These people are talking daily about what's going on in the industry. These are the people you want on your side. If they come across something truly great, you'd better believe they're going to tell their friends about it, which is how an Internet buzz begins.

Now that I had a small customer base, it was time to offer these customers a Second Glass. When I say this, I wasn't going to offer them another product. I was going to essentially refill their glass with the same beverage. Remember, my goal here is to create a product so great that my customers almost feel obligated to tell the world about what they've purchased. It was time to make "Link Proctor" better by adding more features. But how did I know what features to add? I simply asked them, but I knew that in order to get a good response to my question, I would have to provide them with something of value first. Remember, my customer base wasn't very large, so I knew I needed a very high response from my e-mail in order to get a long list of new features.

I spent the next few weeks visiting that original forum, looking at the questions being asked. I then wrote up a 35-page e-book, in Microsoft Word, answering all of those questions asked in the forum. I converted it to e-book format (a PDF document).

Now, rather than just sending it out to my customer base as a free gift, I first had someone who creates nice e-book graphics design a nice-looking graphic for my newly created e-book. People are very visually oriented by nature. If the picture of the e-book looks nice, it instantly increases the value of the product. People will automatically think the e-book is that much better, just by being able to associate a picture with the product.

Next, I sent out an e-mail to all of my customers—which wasn't many back then. In the e-mail I told them I created a very special surprise bonus for them, something they would absolutely love. I directed them to a special web page that I created. On this web page was a picture of the e-book, which I paid someone to create, a couple paragraphs explaining what questions the e-book answered, and exactly how it would help them. The key is making the web page very benefits oriented.

The catch to this whole process was that in order to receive this free e-book, they needed to first e-mail me their wish list of things they wanted to see in the next release of Link Proctor. So, not only do they get a free e-book, but they also get to tell me exactly what they would like the software to do. People love to have a sense of belonging, and knowing that something they recommend would be added to the software gives them that needed sense.

What did I get out of this? Remember, these customers are plugged into the search engine optimization market fairly well, or they wouldn't have seen my ad in the forum. So, by surveying them, I got inside access to people who already know exactly what the market wants. By giving away this free e-book, which cost me roughly $50 (the cost of the graphic), I:

- Made my customers very happy.
- Increased my chances of these customers recommending Link Proctor to others in the forum.
- Got my new features list for Version 2.0.

Now that I had my features list, which had some very good requests that I would have never thought of on my own, I began working on Version 2.0. A month later, I offered them that Second Glass by releasing Version 2.0 of Link Proctor to my customers. (*Note:* If you're selling software or something that can be updated, it's very important to give customers free lifetime upgrades/updates.)

As soon as I released Version 2.0, I immediately began receiving a large amount of thank-you e-mails. Customers couldn't believe I had actually read their minds and given them exactly what they wanted. They didn't realize I'd just given them what customers asked me for. These people then went back to that very same forum and began posting comments about how happy they were with Link Proctor.

A buzz was starting to develop. . . . But we're just getting started.

This was the perfect time to offer them a Third Glass. Now is when I decided to create a members forum for all software users. Remember, as I said earlier, people love to feel a sense of belonging to a group. Having a members forum was just that: I allowed them to feel like they were part of a group. And where did I get the idea to create a members forum? You guessed it. Several customers recommended it when I did that initial survey, where I gave out the free e-book. Surveying customers is a perfect way to find out exactly what to offer them next.

Several more months went by and I paid heavy attention to my members forum. I answered every single question that anyone asked. Within the first several weeks, I had well over 1,000 posts in the forum. This is very important. To get members active in a forum, you have to be very active yourself. Now, how did I use the forum to my advantage? Once the forum started getting pretty active, I did two things.

1. I created a "feature requests section" for Link Proctor.

2. I closely monitored the forum, looking for common questions and concerns.

Remember, it was a forum that led me to my original Thirsty Crowd. Now that I had my very own forum, I would have unlimited access to a plethora of other possible product ideas. Over time, I noticed something people seemed to really want. This was a web site where they could easily find other like-minded people who would want to exchange links with their web site. (This is a search engine optimization tactic. If you don't know what it means, just bear with me.) I also noticed two other products/services that would seem to solve another problem that they seemed to have.

Once I knew this, I knew what it was time for: another survey. This time, I didn't have to give them anything. I could post a survey in my members forum and users could take a few minutes and just select which service they'd be most interested in. A couple of weeks went by, and the landslide winner was "Create a web site where users could go to exchange links with other people." I now had a great back-end product to sell to my current customers, and it was something I was 100 percent certain they would want, because they told me that was what they wanted.

From there, linkmetro.com was created. Theoretically, I could have easily charged for this service, but I knew if I made it free, it would start to create a buzz. And, as I've said, this is something I try to incorporate into every product I create.

So, what have I done so far? I've found a Thirsty Crowd by visiting forums related to my market. I've advertised in one of the forums. Once I built a customer base, I surveyed them to find out exactly what they want more of, less of, and so on. I've given them more than they paid for, in terms of the e-book I wrote specifically for them. I've given them exactly what they asked for, not once, not twice, but three times (software features, members forum, linkmetro.com). That's not just a Second Glass, but a Third Glass as well.

At this point, a real buzz is taking place. Why? Simply because I'm giving them something great, *something to talk about*. Now, you might be wondering why you've never heard of Link Proctor and the answer is this: After the release of Version 2.0, I realized that the features within Version 2.0 no longer matched the name of the product. So, I did yet another survey at another forum—this time, a popular marketing fo-rum. The survey was, "Give me a new name for my software and I'll give the winner a free copy." No skin off my back, and I knew someone was bound to come up with a catchy name.

Several days later, **SEO Elite Version 2.0** was created. For those who aren't knowledgeable about search engine opti-mization, do a Google search for "SEO Elite" and have a look at what you find.

All of this was done by:

1. Seeking a common problem and offering a solution.
2. Surveying customers to find out what they want more of, less of, and so on.
3. Then offering them a Second Glass for free (free soft-ware upgrade and bonus e-book), which gives them something to talk about.

Now that I have a large customer base, I can easily survey them over and over by offering them more free products and gifts. Once I know what they want by surveying them, I can offer them a Second, Third, Fourth, and Fifth Glass of what-ever they want. The possibilities are truly endless.

So, to answer the original question, "What's the secret to completely dominating any market within 180 days?" It's easy—if you follow the three simple steps you'll be well on your way to doing just that: completely dominating your market.

Don't let the simplicity of this example pass you by. It's not just some cutesy way to market your product, but it is very powerful if you can truly grasp the concept. Follow this for-mula and you're sure to succeed.

How to Create Your Own "Thirsty Crowd" from Scratch for Automatic Repeat Profits

Craig Perrine

Craig Perrine, CEO of MaverickMarketer.com, has helped hundreds of entrepreneurs build large, responsive lists in many different niche markets. Craig has the knack of knowing how to explain complex subjects in an easily understandable way. He also knows how to build profitable long-term relationships with targeted subscriber lists and has used these skills to teach private clients and seminar audiences how to use his highly effective methods for more than 10 years. Craig has worked for himself, and with clients both large and small, to generate millions in sales in a variety of markets, including information products, professional services, and software using direct-marketing and direct-selling campaigns. As if all that weren't enough, he also created a best-selling multimedia course that teaches the same methods he uses to build substantial lists of targeted, responsive subscribers, and is highly sought after to speak at exclusive seminars that people willingly pay up to $5,000 to attend!

To learn more about Craig, please visit his web site at www .maverickmarketer.com.

Before you can present The Irresistible Offer and then sell a Second Glass, you have to have a Thirsty Crowd. There are many different ways to identify Thirsty Crowds, but it's going to cost you either time or money or both to do so.

Wouldn't it be great if you could snap your fingers (or click a mouse) and have an instant Thirsty Crowd just waiting to buy from you? If you had such a wonderful thing, anytime you wanted to bring in money you could simply present your offer and sales would pour in as if by magic.

The good news is that you can generate sales out of thin air when you gather your Thirsty Crowd on a list that you can follow up with again and again. How? You offer a *free* report or similar giveaway with high perceived (and real) value to your target market in exchange for their e-mail and/or physical address.

Done correctly, this means you will have permission to follow up with each person who subscribed (or opted in) to your list and be in a position to make an Irresistible Offer as well as sell a Second Glass for as long as they remain your subscribers.

If you try to build a list the wrong way, even a large list will not be very valuable. This is because the very core of a list's value is the relationship between you and your subscriber, and the only reason subscribers stay on your list is if there is value in it for them to do so.

So the questions are, how do you find a Thirsty Crowd? And what do you offer them to build a list?

I've built lists in a variety of niche markets including self-help, Internet marketers, health and fitness, as well as several more obscure markets. And in every case the formula is the same: I thoroughly research what my target subscribers really want and what problems and frustrations they face in getting what they want.

For example, Internet marketers want to learn how to use online strategies, tools, and tactics to promote their businesses and build lists, among other things. They often are new to the Internet in general and need to learn how to harness the vast communication power of reaching a global audience with the click of a mouse. So there are plenty of frustrations and challenges within this niche to solve with products and services of my own and by referring my subscribers to other people's products and services for a commission.

I'm always looking for new ways to discover what my target markets want and to identify new niche markets. Specific tools and tactics come and go, so anything I tell you here may be outdated by the time you read this. For this reason I've posted a web site for you to see my latest suggestions at www.maverickmarketer.com/greatoffer.htm.

But some key strategies are timeless and can be done right quickly and easily from home.

The important principle is to make sure that whatever product or service you are thinking of offering has a Thirsty Crowd waiting for you. The great thing about the Internet is that you can go to places like eBay.com, Amazon.com, Froogle.com, and Half.com, and see what people are buying.

Whether you are selling hard goods like electronics or how-to information products, you should be able to find your niche represented in one of these huge marketplace web sites. If you don't, consider that a major red flag and do careful research before you invest a lot of time and money in that business.

Probably the most powerful online tools for reaching any target market as I write this are Google.com's and Overture.com's pay per click search engines (again, see www.maverickmarketer .com/greatoffer.htm for my current suggestions). While most people know you can get your web site found in the search engines and be discovered, it is also a complex and ever-changing game to have your web site be in the top page when someone searches.

Pay per click allows you to simply pay to be in the top search results for any keywords you choose. There is an art and a science to pay per click that goes beyond the scope of our topic today but you can see that if you can get in front of a lot of people who are searching online for what you have to sell, you could put up a web site offering a freebie in exchange for an e-mail address and build a very targeted list.

If I want to sell a book on training German shepherd dogs to be great family pets and scary guard dogs as well I could offer a free report called "How to Train Your German shepherd to Be a Lovable Guard Dog" and drive pay per click traffic to that page. Visitors then would find a simple web site that describes my free offer and a form to enter their name and e-mail address to get a copy.

This is called a "landing page" and is the cornerstone of gathering the subscription information from your visitors.

The challenge with pay per click and search engines is that for the beginning Internet marketer it can be complex and expensive to learn how to cost-effectively use that strategy to build a list, especially because if you pay too much per click you might find that it takes too long to make your money back from the subscribers you get.

If you want to use this strategy but don't want to become a pay per click search engine expert, you can hire people to do the hard part for you. Again, look to my resource page mentioned earlier for a current recommendation for pursuing this strategy and also for home study courses on how to do it yourself if you are interested.

One way that I consistently get traffic to my sites and new subscribers to my list is actually simple and in most cases free. I write (or pay someone to write) articles and submit them to e-zine publishers and web sites looking for content on specific subjects. Again, the exact resources for this will change, so go to www.maverickmarketer.com/greatoffer.com for up-to-date recommendations on where to submit your articles to get the right exposure.

But here is the strategy that will never go out of style. People search the Internet for content, and if they find an article by you that answers their question on a particular topic and offers more information at your web site, they'll view you as a credible expert and go see what you have to offer.

The great part about this is that these visitors will come to your landing page that I described earlier and have to register or subscribe to get the further information that you offer beyond what they found in the free article. You can promise them a free download of an e-book (which can simply be a collection of related articles) or a subscription to your newsletter if you like. Either way, you are getting a targeted subscriber who views you as an expert using this method of list building.

We perceive authors (including article authors) as experts, and as long as you deliver useful content (which you can pay someone else peanuts to dig up for you using the resources I list for you at my site), new subscribers will respect your recommendations and be more likely to buy from you than if they simply found your sales page instead.

The formula for writing an article is to pick a subject that you know is of interest to your target market. For example, if you know people are concerned about having their German shepherd dogs attack people who are not intruders, you could then create an article on how to make your German shepherd people friendly while still being a loyal and effective guard dog.

Specific topics like this are better than trying to write all about dogs. Give good content on one specific topic and then tell your reader that for more information they can visit your web site or subscribe to your free newsletter. You don't want to write huge, long articles, either. Just give enough information to cover your specific topic and then generate curiosity in your readers so they visit your site for more information. Ultimately, the nitty-gritty in-depth how-to information will be found in the products you have for sale, so the whole point of this process is to give enough information away to build credibility and a trusting relationship with your visitors but let them know that if they want you to provide your full expertise they will have to pay you.

A key principle to understand here is that you are building credibility, trust, and a relationship with your visitors and turning them into subscribers by giving value before you ask them to buy anything. Your whole goal here is to make an Irresistible Offer strong enough to get them on your list so you can follow up with them over and over again. In a real sense, you are building your own Thirsty Crowd by offering a taste of water and then selling them a whole glass and a Second Glass and so on once they trust you.

Remember, I said in the beginning that your list would be only as valuable as the relationship you develop with your subscriber. Part of that is trust, of course, but part of it is that you need to get paid for the value you are providing at some point or you don't have a business at all.

So just remember that you give away a taste of water to prove you have the goods but you then offer a glass for sale if they want a full drink. They'll soon understand that they can't get everything they want from just a taste and that's part of the strategy from the beginning.

Let's walk through a scenario I've used over and over to convert people from a taste to a First Glass and then a Second Glass and so on.

The key is to make a gradual transition from giving away free to getting paid so you don't shock your subscriber. Because your first-time Web visitor doesn't know you yet and has a lot of other choices that are but a mouse click away, you want to offer your taste of what they want up front for little or no money. This removes any risk on their part in checking you out, and it separates you from most of your competition who don't use this tactic.

Now, if I gave away a report on how to raise a German shepherd puppy to be a great family dog and guard dog, too, I am in a good position to get someone who has tried this taste of my content to subscribe to my newsletter about German shepherds.

Once I have that foothold in the relationship with my new subscriber, I can then offer a low-priced product for sale—something that costs enough to make me some money but not too much, so they can feel if they don't like it that they haven't risked much. In my experience, this is usually between $19.95 and $39.95. In this example, I might have a book about other topics of interest to German shepherd owners, such as potty training, how to get your dog to heel, how to keep dogs off the furniture, how to stop them from chewing your shoes, and so forth. This would be the First Glass product they buy from me.

Next, I want to sell them a Second Glass, and since I have established trust and value at this point, I might as well ask for more money for a bigger, more in-depth product such as a complete A-to-Z home study course with audio and video that clearly demonstrates how to do all the steps in the mini-reports or First Glass type products. This home study course would probably cost anywhere from $97 to $997, depending on the market, and would be the big profit generator and Second Glass for your business.

You can see where running an ad online to sell a $997 course would not get as much of a response as offering a free e-book or newsletter and building up trust, because a whole lot more people will take advantage of a free offer than will spring several hundred dollars on an offer from a stranger.

This brings me to my favorite Thirsty Crowd list-building technique. As with your subscribers, I've found that the greatest opportunity to reach out and leverage your business by partnering with other people who also market in your niche is by developing trusted relationships.

So far, the process I've been describing has involved building a trusted relationship with your own Thirsty Crowd on your list. You can imagine that other people who have established businesses and are well beyond the Second Glass with their subscribers are in a position to recommend your products and generate sales for you. This is called a joint venture, and it is by far my favorite and most used list-building technique.

For example, earlier this year, working with a network or other key players I launched a home study course on list building by partnering with influential marketers in my Internet marketing niche, and we generated over six figures in sales in the first couple of weeks. This would have been far more difficult if not impossible to do just by myself and is a great illustration of the power of networking with complementary businesses in your niche.

If you've been creating tastes of what you have to offer in the form of articles, e-books, newsletters, and so forth, you are in a great position to network with people with lists and offer to give a taste to their lists in exchange for sharing any profits that come in with the list owner.

I do this all the time in the form of offering bonuses for my business friends to add on to their offers to their customers. The only rule of thumb is that you have to be offering something of value as an Irresistible Offer to your joint venture partner's list not only to prove your value but also to help your partner look good to their list. From the subscriber's point of view, your joint venture partner is adding value to them by introducing another source of useful content so it's truly a win-win situation all around if done correctly.

The main advantage to you in doing this is that your joint venture partner has already built trust and credibility with their list and when they recommend you or your taste to their subscribers that trust transfers to you. Often you will find you can skip the freebie and move right to the First Glass product so that you and your partner immediately profit from any sales. In the right circumstances, you could even give away your First Glass product as part of a special promotion of your bigger Second Glass if the joint venture partner feels it would be a good fit.

You can see the power of this because you essentially leapfrog from being a stranger to your joint venture partner's Thirsty Crowd to being a recommended resource in a position to profit immediately. The trick to this is that you must prove yourself to your joint venture partner first before they would be willing to risk their reputation on you. My best advice for establishing potential joint venture relationships is to get out to live events like seminars and conferences related to your niche and meet people in person and establish friendships with them. Then you'll be in a position to know what they would be interested in offering and be able to prove your credibility in a live environment.

If that is not an option for you, I would go to Google and find the web sites that come up in your niche and one by one use phone or e-mail to contact potential joint venture partners directly that way. I'd suggest sending an e-mail and following up with a phone call if possible. You'll be surprised at how effective this can be if you are prepared to offer proof that there is a good fit between your products and theirs.

Of course, in the space available here I haven't had enough room to explain everything there is to know about warming up a relationship with your new Thirsty Crowd list, but I've shown you the surest path to profits that has proven very profitable for myself and my joint venture partners.

I invite you to check out my popular free seven-part e-course on exactly how to build that profitable relationship with your list at www.maverickmarketer.com. You can watch me implement each of the techniques I have shared with you and more that we haven't had time for here.

In any case, remember to check out the updated resource page I've created at www.maverickmarketer.com/greatoffer.htm to take advantage of the resources you'll need to use the strategies I've shared with you today (you can sign up for the e-course there as well).

Here's to your online profits.

Getting Others to "Pass the Glass": Ethics and the Success Stream

Shel Horowitz

Shel Horowitz is an award-winning copywriter, publishing/marketing consultant, and author. He got his start in marketing back in the 1970s, volunteering for community issue groups that were so poor there wasn't even enough in the budget to buy stamps—so Shel would deliver the press releases using his bicycle. Since 1981, Shel has offered afford-able copywriting and marketing/publishing consulting services. Working from an antique farmhouse in rural Massachusetts, he has helped clients on three continents focus their messages and reach their key audiences. His two most recent books are Principled Profit: Marketing That Puts People First *(Accurate Writing More, 2003) and* Grassroots Marketing: Getting Noticed in a Noisy World *(Chelsea Green, 2000).*

Shel is also the founder of the Ethical Business Pledge movement at www.principledprofits.com/25000influencers.html.

For more information about Shel and the concepts he discusses here, you can visit www.frugalmarketing.com.

FIND THE THIRSTY CUSTOMER

Finding customers is a simple three-step process:

1. Identify a market need/desire.
2. Figure out how you can meet that need with something you love doing and do really well.

3. Determine how to reach this market, and with what message.

Okay, so if it's that simple, why is marketing such a tough challenge for so many entrepreneurs? Because most "marketers" go about it all backward. They think first about what they like to do, then they develop a product, and only then do they scramble around looking for a market. And then, they blow it completely with a "me, me, me" marketing message. Any sales they get are in spite of their marketing, and not because of it (ouch!).

But it's not about the marketer. It's about the *prospect*— about his or her needs, desires, problems. It's about being of service to others, and using that service attitude to succeed. It may sound trite, but it's about being nice—about building on-going relationships. And its about being completely honest and ethical in your search for the perfect fit between you and a prospect, even if it means turning down a project.

In a panel on sales and marketing, I had to follow an aggressive, rude, and arrogant sales jerk. His advice was to pick up the phone and cold-call aggressively, hour after hour, day after day. His theory seemed to be that if you were a thorn in the side of enough people, one or two of them would do business with you, just to get rid of you.

With his approach, everyone loses. He's going to have to work 14 hours a day at alienating people in order to make a decent living. He's wasting a lot of effort that could be spent far more productively, and he's destroying the chance to build the long-lasting, positive relationships that turn prospects not just into customers, but into ambassadors for you.

When I finally got the floor, I said, "Now, here's the difference between marketing and sales. I never make cold calls. I create marketing that has the prospect calling me! When I get the phone call or the e-mail, they're already convinced that I can help them. If I don't screw it up, I have the account." This is actually the dominant marketing trend in my business.

Wouldn't you like prospects to beg you, "Please work with me"? When you approach your business with the mind-set of service and ethics—and combine that with powerful marketing strategies that position you as the best solution to your prospect's problem—that's exactly what will happen.

So . . . how can you actually find the people who are desperately thirsty for your offer?

There are dozens and dozens of ways. Here are a few of my favorites—and you'll notice that these methods cost nothing but time—and in some cases (speaking, writing) actually *generate revenue directly*:

- Build referrals (or at least testimonials) from industry experts, ordinary customers, and even your competitors.

- Speak to audiences that include your best markets.

- Specialize in a few narrow market sectors, small enough to brand yourself effectively but large enough to supply a critical mass of prospects, where you can become the go-to person.

- Participate actively *and helpfully* in a few carefully chosen Internet discussion groups, including a "sig" (signature file) that briefly sums up how you can help people and offers a concrete reason to visit your web site.

- Submit problem-solving articles to e-zines, web sites, printed magazines, and newsletters.

- Write a useful book, and market it effectively (be sure to include your own capabilities and contact information).

- Become a recognized expert by hosting your own radio or television show, teleclass series, blog, and/or Podcast.

Sometimes you can accomplish amazing things by thinking creatively about how to harness this attitude of service and ethics. As an example, I started a worldwide campaign to create a "tipping point" toward ethical business. My long-term goal is to change the business climate to the point where the next Enron or Tyco scandal would be as unthinkable tomorrow as slavery is today. I probably would not have come up with this if I hadn't been thinking about ways to spread my sixth book, *Principled Profit: Marketing That Puts People First*, to different audiences. To move this idea forward, I started the Business Ethics Pledge campaign, at www.principledprofits.com/25000influencers.html. My goal is to change the business culture by getting 25,000 business leaders to sign on over 10 years, each of whom will inform at least 100 more people (easy to do, and I provide a dozen ways).

From doing this campaign,

- I've been hired as a paid columnist for *Business Ethics* magazine—which means I receive a check in order to mention my book title and the pledge four times a year to my exact target audience: people who can hire me to speak or to write for them, and who might potentially buy bulk quantities of my book.

- People have gone out of their way to introduce me to others who will be helpful in this campaign, and they are also helpful in my career (this includes some of the top names in the marketing world).

- The campaign gave me an opening to approach newsletter publishers and planners at prestigious conferences, who have publicized my work to several hundred thousand people I wouldn't have reached on my own.

- It may have been a factor in reselling my book to foreign publishers, and in getting a slot on a local station to do my radio show.

- And yes, I can definitely trace quite a few book sales to individuals who have signed the pledge.

OFFERING THE SECOND GLASS—AND GETTING THE GLASS PASSED AROUND

One of the most effective ways to build an ethical business is to go back to people who already know you, whose thirst for knowledge or solutions or happiness you've already helped to slake, and to offer them, in Mark Joyner's words, "a Second Glass."

On average, it costs a business five times as much to bring in a new customer as to bring back a previous one. So that means, if you're working through traditional (expensive) marketing approaches, *every customer you bring back saves you 80 percent of your marketing cost* to acquire a fresh customer.

Until a few years ago, my typical customer would come in with a one-time need, spend $100 or $200, and that would be it. So I was constantly in marketing mode.

Since embracing the concept of the Second Glass, without really shifting my marketing methods, and certainly without spending any extra marketing dollars, I've been able to land a number of clients who are with me for many months at a time, doing numerous projects together. Instead of getting, say, a single press release, now my typical client gets a series of press releases; copy for some web site pages, direct-mail letters, or sell sheets; and a personalized marketing plan. A few have even turned to me for start-to-finish consulting about how to take a raw, unedited manuscript and develop it into a polished and marketable book.

And this is great—but there's one more piece, and that's getting others to pass the glass around for you. Recommendations by others are far more powerful than anything you can say about yourself. Even better, when you get a new client through referral, you haven't had to reach into your wallet. *Your cost to acquire this new customer is zero.*

In my own business, I enjoy a steady stream of referrals from industry experts. Several of them list me as a preferred vendor in their books and on their web sites. Some ask for a commission, which I'm happy to pay; after all, it's still going to cost me far less and be much easier to complete the sale than if I approach a prospect cold, out of the blue. Others just prefer to accumulate so-called karma points, because they know the value to their own customers in sending them away happy, in serving that client's needs and desires and therefore making it much more likely that the client will return.

And of course, karma is a big part of it. I frequently recommend other vendors to people, and in this way, I build the circle—whether or not those referrals go to the same people who are referring clients to me. I'm totally convinced that if I didn't do this, I wouldn't receive many referrals.

One final related heresy: I don't believe I have competitors, and I don't pay much attention to market share. The world is an abundant place, and there's far more copywriting out there than I could ever take on. So I'm delighted that when someone comes to me with a project that isn't right for me, I have a place to refer. I even list 20 of my supposed competitors (or marketing partners, as I prefer to think of them) in the back of my book, with full contact information, web sites, and areas of specialization. And I know that karma will come back to me, many times over. The more I embrace abundance in my life and in my worldview, the more the world reveals to me that it is, indeed, an abundant place—and that the more I live my life and my work in harmony with the "Magic Triangle" principles of honesty, integrity, and quality, the more the universe rewards me.

I explore these concepts in much greater detail in my award-winning fifth and sixth books, *Grassroots Marketing: Getting Noticed in a Noisy World* (www.frugalmarketing.com) and *Principled Profit: Marketing That Puts People First* (www.principledprofits.com). I invite you to sign the Business Ethics Pledge at www.principledprofits.com/25000influencers.html.

How to Find a Thirsty Crowd on Google

Perry Marshall

Perry Marshall is an author, speaker, and consultant in Chicago. He is known as "The Wizard of Google AdWords" and is one of the world's leading specialists on buying search engine traffic. Google advertisers who use his methods generate over half a billion clicks per month (conservative estimate). His company, Perry S. Marshall & Associates, consults both online and brick-and-mortar companies on generating sales leads, increasing Web traffic, and getting maximum advertising results.

If you would like to find out more about Perry, his web site is at www.perrymarshall.com.

During the past five years, the very direction of marketing and advertising has made a complete reversal. And that means it has never been easier to access a Thirsty Crowd than it is right now! In this article I show you how to find a Thirsty Crowd instantly with the world's most popular search engine, Google.

Let me start by telling you about a marketing genius whom most people have never heard of, and his brilliant Internet insight.

The name Lester Wunderman may not be familiar to you, but you've undoubtedly benefited from his innovations. Wunderman devised some of the most innovative marketing campaigns of all time, including the Columbia Record and Tape

Club, the Book of the Month Club, and the American Express Card. In his book *Being Direct* (Direct Marketing Association, 2004), he describes how he developed marketing practices that were radical years ago but standard today.

At a speech in 1999, Wunderman explained that before the Internet, salespeople had a prospect list and were chasing the customers. With the Internet, the prospect list has changed hands. Now customers are coming after the salespeople. He said that until marketers and salespeople recognize this fundamental shift, business as usual will be tough sledding.

That's why some businesses are struggling mightily, yet others are experiencing tremendous success, giving glasses of water to thirsty customers as fast as they can fill them. The biggest difference is this reversal. It's not about the salespeople chasing the customers; it's about figuring what the customers are looking for and putting it in front of them!

As simple as that may sound, most companies are totally missing this. And it's not voodoo magic. The tools are readily available, and you just need to use them with an extra bit of finesse.

Let's say you sell saltshakers. How would you sell them before the Internet?

There's no such thing as a saltshaker store, so you'd have to go to retailers and catalogs and get them to place orders with you. It might take months before your product is being rung up at the cash register.

But on the Internet, there are people searching for saltshakers *right now*. You can sell them a saltshaker *today*.

Now for saltshakers, there's probably not a huge number searching. But people *are* searching. I looked it up on Overture's handy keyword research tool (http://inventory.overture .com) and found that Overture is getting about 30,000 searches a month. Google probably gets more.

If you search for "saltshakers" on Google you get this result:

Google™ Web Images Groups News Froogle Local^{New!} more »

[salt shakers] [Search] Advanced Search Preferences

Web   Results 1 - 10 of about 1,950,000 for salt shakers. (0.27 seconds)

CHEF'S: Official Site   Sponsored Links   Sponsored Links
www.chefscatalog.com   Brand Name Kitchen Bakeware, Tools Electronics & More up to 70% off!

Salt Shakers   Tabletools.com
www.Williams-Sonoma.com   Browse a wide array of salt and pepper mills at Williams-Sonoma.   Large assortment of pepper mills,
                                                                                 salt shakers, and more!
Salt shakers For Less   www.tabletools.com
InsideKitchen.com/SaltShakers   "Top Quality" Food Service Supplies Deep Discounts & Fast Shipping!
                                                                                 Salt Shakers
News results for **salt shakers** - View today's top stories   Find, compare and buy Kitchen!
  MY FAVORITE THING/Salt-and-pepper shakers - Newsday - 16 minutes ago   Simply Fast Savings
                                                                                 www.Shopping.com

Salt Shakers Inc. | Welcome to Salt Shakers!   Salt Shakers
Salt Shakers is a Christian ethics action group based in Melbourne Australia, focussing on   Bargain Prices.
building awareness in the Australian Church of issues of ethical ...   You want it, we got it!
www.saltshakers.org.au/ - 40k - Cached - Similar pages   BizRate.com

The Messianic world. Saltshakers messianic community: Where Jews ...   Salt Shakers
The messianic world with the Saltshakers Messianic Community for news, views and prayer   Up to 70% Off Restaurant Supplies.
for Israel, an introduction to the Christian gospel for Jews and a ...   Live Help & Secure Site. Free S&H!
www.saltshakers.com/ - 36k - Cached - Similar pages   www.Instawares.com

Pepper & Salt Shakers   Mikasa French Countryside
Salt and pepper shakers in a variety of sizes and shapes.   White Stoneware Salt and Pepper Set
fantes.com/pepper_salt_shakers.htm - 43k - Cached - Similar pages   Only $19.99 (or order used).
                                                                                 Amazon.com

On your computer screen, the colored bands across the top and the ads going down the right side are paid listings. As an advertiser, you bid on keywords (like "salt and pepper shaker") and pay when your prospective customer clicks on your ad and goes to your site.

This is the first time in the history of advertising that you could advertise specifically to customers who are looking for what you sell, right now, and you pay only when they show up to find out what you have to say!

That's the huge reversal that Lester Wunderman was talking about. It's not about what we marketers want to sell; it's about what our customers want to buy. It's about what they're *thirsty* for.

In the old days, market research usually meant going around to a bunch of stores and seeing what brands were selling and checking the prices, surveying customers, and investigating manufacturers' sales figures.

All that is still just as valuable as it ever was, but the Internet gives us up-to-date data on what people are searching for.

KEYWORD RESEARCH = YOUR "THIRSTY CROWD RADAR SCREEN"

Now you can do keyword research and find out what's popular—what's hot *right now*—and find a way to capitalize on Thirsty Crowds.

Let me show you a few fun ways to find Thirsty Crowds.

One example is Google's Zeitgeist (www.google.com/press/ zeitgeist.html), which tells you which keywords have gained and lost popularity during the current week:

Zeitgeist This Week
Top 15 Gaining Queries:
Week Ending October 24, 2005

1. hurricane wilma
2. madonna
3. national hurricane center
4. NOAA
5. britney spears baby
6. jennifer aniston
7. powerball
8. cancun
9. quake 4
10. batman begins
11. world series
12. doom
13. saw
14. pumpkin carving patterns
15. charlize theron

Each of these items is a market. I'm doing this search at the end of October, and notice "pumpkin carving patterns" shows up at number 14. Now, just because it's on this list doesn't mean you can make money from it, but it definitely tells you what's hot, what people are searching for.

Here are some other interesting things from Zeitgeist:

Tech Toys
September 2005

1. psp
2. ipod nano
3. winmx

225

4. <u>nintendo revolution</u>
5. <u>mp3 music download</u>

Top Worries
September 2005

1. <u>hurricane</u>
2. <u>bird flu</u>
3. <u>gas prices</u>
4. <u>phishing</u>
5. <u>housing bubble</u>

Do you see thirst in these lists? I sure do!

Let's take a look at another resource, Wordtracker (www .wordtracker.info). Wordtracker has a list of the top 1,000 keywords on the Internet. Here's a sampling, numbers 37 to 55:

37	50 cent	50249
38	playstation 2 cheats	49409
39	family guy	49291
40	jokes	48812
41	thong	48666
42	jennifer lopez	48539
43	angelina jolie	48356
44	my chemical romance	48166
45	kds bbs pics	48098
46	names	47638
47	inuyasha	46582
48	cars	45918
49	hotmail.com	45889
50	free radio stations	45819
51	weather	45114
52	eminem	44622

53	teen	44583
54	fall out boy	44386
55	bikini	43852

With any of these keywords, you can go to Google, click on "Advertising Programs," write an ad, type in the keyword, set a bid price, and pay Google $5, and your ad can be showing anywhere in the world within 10 minutes.

A WORD OF CAUTION

If you go about doing this willy-nilly, it can be a formula for losing a lot of money really fast. You need to know what you're doing (Google bidding strategies, writing persuasive and targeted ads), and your web site needs to effectively sell or generate sales leads.

But even if you just decide to spend a few bucks to see what happens, you can learn a lot about people and what they're searching for. Here's a short list:

- You can use the Overture tool (http://inventory.overture .com) to find out exactly what kinds of words and variations of phrases people are typing in. For example, Overture shows 852 searches for "antique salt and pepper shaker." That's a valuable piece of information.

- You can buy some traffic, and even if you don't have a web site yet, you can send it to someone else's web site, just to see how much traffic there is and exactly how much it costs.

- You can see exactly what other advertisers are selling to the same Thirsty Crowd. Notice, for example, the different kinds of ads that show up in the "salt shakers" search. The savvy marketer asks: Is there a need that's not being filled here?

- You can create not one but multiple ads, and see which ones get better responses. Tiny word changes can make *huge* differences. Here are two examples:

  Easy Self-Defense for Ordinary People
  Fast Personal Protection Training
  www.tftgroup.com
  0.6 percent CTR

  Simple Self-Defense for Ordinary People
  Easy Personal Protection Training
  www.tftgroup.com
  1.1 percent CTR

"CTR" stands for click-through-rate, the percentage of people who searched and saw the ad, and actually clicked on that ad.

Only two words changed: Easy/Simple in the first line and Fast/Easy in the second line. But the response is almost double for the second ad, compared to the first! In Google this is really important, because in Google's system the better ad will cost half as much for the same position.

So with these simple tools you can now quickly find out:

- A huge list of things people are thirsty for (Eminem or Playstation 2 Cheats).
- Nuances of what people are thirsty for (saltshakers vs. antique salt and pepper shakers).
- What thirsty people click on ("easy self-defense" vs. "simple self-defense").

You don't have to build it and hope they come. You find where they're going and build it right there. And hand out those glasses of water as fast as you can fill 'em.

If you'd like to learn more about Google AdWords—and some of the subtle tricks you need to know to play the game right—go to www.perrymarshall.com/google and sign up for my free five-day e-mail course.

How to Access Pent-up Demand, Create New Value, and Get the Quantum Leap Upsell: The True Story of a Million-Dollar Idea

Perry Marshall

I f you slog your way through some dreary economics textbook, one of the first things they'll tell you about is the supply-demand thing. They drone on about it as though the price of your product and the demand for it comprise a simple, one-dimensional thing. But the savvy marketing alchemist knows: *Nothing could be further from the truth!*

The savvy marketer knows that people have a vast range of appetites for just about anything. Take music, for example: There are some people who wouldn't go to a Rolling Stones concert if you paid 'em 500 bucks. There are other people who will follow the band across the country and pay 500 bucks to sit in the front row at every single concert from Boston to San Francisco.

And of course there is every interest level in between, from the guy who just likes to occasionally hear "You can't get what you want" on the radio to the couple who has a few Stones albums and goes to a concert for the first time, just to see what it's like.

INFORMATION AND SERVICES: ENORMOUS PRICE RANGES

When you sell information, professional services, or anything that's personality driven (i.e., author, speaker, consultant, musician, actor), the range of prices that people will pay for you is *enormous*. The average guy on the street might not pay one thin dime for your advice, while there may be a handful of people who would pay thousands, tens of thousands, or even hundreds of thousands of dollars for your help.

You can use Mark Joyner's Second Glass technique to find out who won't pay . . . and who will and how much. The savvy marketer lets the customers sort themselves out. This reduces your marketing cost by a huge amount and grows your profit margins dramatically.

CASUAL CONVERSATION UNCOVERS A MILLION-DOLLAR MISSED OPPORTUNITY

I was at a seminar talking to my friend Bill Harrison of Free Publicity.com and he said, "Hey, Perry, I bought your Google AdWords book and it's really great, but I'm probably implementing only one-tenth of the stuff in there, and what I really need is a kick in the butt and some hands-on guidance so I'll do it the right way."

Bill continued, "I bet you have a lot of customers with that very same problem. Have you ever thought about starting a coaching program? I bet a lot of people would go for that."

And then he added, "I think it would be a million-dollar idea, Perry. I think it's that good. People are giving Google a lot more money than they need to—nobody knows that better than you."

Bill really got me thinking. I made him sit down with me and I quizzed him about how to put it together, what to charge for it, what it would consist of. We got all the ideas on the table and I was starting to get excited about it. "Hmm, maybe this *is* a million-dollar idea," I said.

"THERE'S JUST ONE CATCH"

Then Bill said, "Now, Perry, if it is, there's just one catch. If this turns out to be a million-dollar idea, you have to donate $10,000 to Cornerstone Christian Academy, which is an inner-city school in Philadelphia. I used to be on their board of directors, and they're doing a lot of really good things. If this is as big as I think it is, I want you to make a donation."

I live in Chicago, so I know what inner-city schools are up against—that sounded like a cause to me (and a small price to pay for a million-dollar idea). So on January 18, I launched *personal AdWords coaching*. Most of my customers had spent as little as $49 to buy my *Definitive Guide to Google AdWords*, and most of them had never bought anything else.

MAKING THE PROMISE MATCH THE PRICE POINT

Personal AdWords coaching promised three things: (1) It's fairly expensive, from $2,500 to $6,000 per seat, but if you meet the qualifications and are accepted, you'll recoup the investment in cost savings and product sales by the end of the course. (2) I offer a money-back guarantee on results: If you take the course and don't increase your income by at least $25,000 within a year, you can get your money back. (3) We're not just going to work on your Google ads; we're going to help you set up testing and tracking, autoresponder messages, e-mail marketing, sales copy—all the ingredients of your sales process.

PENT-UP DEMAND—TO THE TUNE OF $100,000 IN ONE DAY

Bill turned out to be right. I sent out an e-mail blast and had more than $100,000 worth of coaching applications by the end of the next day. There was *pent-up demand* in my list—out of thousands of customers, there were several dozen who were willing and able to invest in this much more expensive program.

That makes perfect sense, if you think about it. I have customers who spend $5,000 to $10,000 a month just buying Google traffic; I have a few who spend over $100,000 a month. One guy I spoke to recently spends $16,000 *per day*.

For those people, a $49 or $97 e-book doesn't scratch the itch—no matter how good it is! Let's say they spend $5,000 a month on traffic. They buy the book, read it, and cut their traffic cost by 20 percent (which is not unusual). Now they save $1,000 a month, every month.

What if they could cut their cost another 20 percent by getting personal coaching, an extra set of eyes and ears? Would it be worth a few thousand dollars to save another $1,000 a month? Often we figure out how to do that on the very first phone call.

People who are investing money in a business (or in education, or in investments, or in a house or a car) are automatically a Thirsty Crowd, if they believe their money can be put to better use than it is right now.

And . . . if the coaching helps them increase their sales— which is what we spent most of our coaching time working on —that is even better.

The lesson here is that selling at just one or two price points can never match the range of appetites within your customer list. If that's all you're doing, you're leaving most of the money on the table. In fact one of the things I teach in coaching is to offer a variety of services at a very wide range of price points so you have something for those elite customers. Because some people are thirstier than others.

THE QUESTION YOU SHOULD ASK YOURSELF

Ask yourself "What would an elite, super-deluxe version of my product look like?" For authors, that can be speaking engagements, coaching programs, or consulting assignments where the author physically does the job for the client. In the case of authors, a $14.95 book in the bookstore is almost certainly *not* the end product; the money from that is usually insignificant. The book is just a front end for another product or service.

You shouldn't think in terms of a deluxe version that's 20 percent more or twice as much. That's helpful, but it's not where the quantum leap is. You should think in terms of a completely expanded service that's literally 10 times or 100 times as much. If you have a significant number of customers, there are a few—maybe just a handful—who will take the elite version.

Do the math, though, and you'll likely discover that there's as much money to be made serving a handful of elite customers as there is serving hundreds or thousands of ordinary ones.

BILL GETS HIS DONATION

I haven't sold a million dollars' worth of coaching yet, but we did pass the half-million dollar mark earlier this year. I wrote a check to Bill's school for $5,000. And I was happy to do it, because I believe in what they're doing, and I sure appreciate Bill's excellent suggestion!

THIS WORKS IN ALMOST ANY MARKET

The coffee shop that sells a $900 cappuccino machine or two every week in addition to the $2 cups of coffee . . . the guy who buys your $18 book at Borders and hires you to do $55,000 of consulting work . . . the $250 passes to meet the

233

band backstage before the concert . . . the United Airlines Red Carpet club . . . the National Republican Senatorial Inner Circle . . . the American Express Centurion card . . . all of these are examples of the exact same idea. How can you engineer your business for a quantum leap upsell?

Think of it like this: The Second Glass doesn't have to be the same size as the first one. It can be a great big jug, or maybe even a fire hose! I bet you've got a few customers who will jump at the chance to get it.

INDEX

Index

Index

How to Quickly Master The Great Formula

15-Minute-Day "Praxis" Gives Total Mastery of Your Business, Time, Energy, and Money

Dear Reader,

Is this you?

You want the record-shattering profits The Great Formula will give, but where do you begin?

As we discussed in Chapter 2, you are bombarded with exabytes of data and the only way to cope is to "chunk" data in useful ways.

The Great Formula allows you to chunk your marketing and that's great, but before you can do that you need to "chunk" your life.

How is it done? With "Simpleology."

Learn how this FREE 18-day course/gadget has changed the lives of over 50,000 people across the globe:

http://www.simpleology.com

Click the link and I'll see you there! MJ

Mark Joyner
South Miami Beach